THE CELL

THE
newbiology

THE CELL

Evolution of the First Organism

Joseph Panno, Ph.D.

Facts On File, Inc.

THE CELL: Evolution of the First Organism

Facts On File, Inc.
132 West 31st Street
New York NY 10001

Library of Congress Cataloging-in-Publication Data
Panno, Joseph.
  The cell : evolution of the first organism / Joseph Panno.
    p. cm. — (New biology)
Includes bibliographical references and index.
  ISBN 0-8160-4946-7 (alk. paper)
  1. Cells—Popular works. 2. Cells—Evolution—Popular works. I. Title.
QH582.4.P36 2004
571.6—dc222003025841

Facts On File books are available at special discounts when purchased in bulk quantities for businesses, associations, institutions or sales promotions. Please call our Special Sales Department in New York at (212) 967-8800 or (800) 322-8755.

You can find Facts On File on the World Wide Web at http://www.factsonfile.com

Text design by Erika K. Arroyo
Cover design by Kelly Parr
Illustrations by Sholto Ainslie and Joseph Panno

Printed in the United States of America

MP FOF 10 9 8 7 6 5 4 3 2

This book is printed on acid-free paper.

For my wife, Diana,
who worked with me in the lab for many years,
and for my daughter Eleanor,
who knew about cells before she could read or write.

∞

CONTENTS

✂

PREFACE

The New Biology set consists of the following six volumes: *The Cell, Animal Cloning, Stem Cell Research, Gene Therapy, Cancer,* and *Aging.* The set is intended primarily for middle and high school students, but it is also appropriate for first-year university students and the general public. In writing this set, I have tried to balance the need for a comprehensive presentation of the material, covering many complex fields, against the danger of burying—and thereby losing—young students under a mountain of detail. Thus the use of lengthy discussions and professional jargon has been kept to a minimum, and every attempt has been made to ensure that this be done without sacrificing the important elements of each topic. A large number of drawings are provided throughout the series to illustrate the subject matter.

The term *new biology* was coined in the 1970s with the introduction of recombinant DNA technology (or biotechnology). At that time, biology was largely a descriptive science in danger of going adrift. Microbiologists at the turn of the century had found cures for a few diseases, and biologists in the 1960s had cracked the genetic code, but there was still no way to study the function of a gene or the cell as a whole. Biotechnology changed all that, and scientists of the period referred to it as the new technique or the new biology. However, since that time it has become clear that the advent of biotechnology was only the first step toward a new biology, a biology that now includes nuclear transfer technology (animal cloning), gene therapy, and stem cell therapy. All these technologies are covered in the six volumes of this set.

The cell is at the very heart of the new biology and thus figures prominently in this book series. Biotechnology was specifically designed for studying cells, and using those techniques, scientists gained insights into cell structure and function that came with unprecedented detail.

As knowledge of the cell grew, the second wave of technologies—animal cloning, stem cell therapy, and gene therapy—began to appear throughout the 1980s and 1990s. The technologies and therapies of the new biology are now being used to treat a wide variety of medical disorders, and someday they may be used to repair a damaged heart, a severed spinal cord, and perhaps even reverse the aging process. These procedures are also being used to enhance food crops and the physical characteristics of dairy cows and to create genetically modified sheep that produce important pharmaceuticals. The last application alone could save millions of lives every year.

While the technologies of the new biology have produced some wonderful results, some of the procedures are very controversial. The ability to clone an animal or genetically engineer a plant raises a host of ethical questions and environmental concerns. Is a cloned animal a freak that we are creating for our entertainment, or is there a valid medical reason for producing such animals? Should we clone ourselves, or use the technology to re-create a loved one? Is the use of human embryonic stem cells to save a patient dying from leukemia a form of high-tech cannibalism? These and many other questions are discussed throughout the series.

The New Biology set is laid out in a specific order, indicated previously, that reflects the natural progression of the discipline. That is, knowledge of the cell came first, followed by animal cloning, stem cell therapy, and gene therapy. These technologies were then used to expand our knowledge of, and develop therapies for, cancer and aging. Although it is recommended that *The Cell* be read first, this is not essential. Volumes 2 through 6 contain extensive background material, located in the final chapter, on the cell and other new biology topics. Consequently, the reader may read the set in the order he or she prefers.

ACKNOWLEDGMENTS

I would first like to thank my friend and mentor, the late Dr. Karun Nair, for helping me understand some of the intricacies of the biological world and for encouraging me to seek that knowledge by looking beyond the narrow confines of any one discipline. The clarity and accuracy of the initial manuscript for this book was greatly improved by reviews and comments from Diana Dowsley and Michael Panno, and later by Frank Darmstadt, Executive Editor; Dorothy Cummings, Project Editor; and Anthony Sacramone, Copy Editor. I am also indebted to Ray Spangenburg, Kit Moser, Sharon O'Brien, and Diana Dowsley for their help in locating photographs for the New Biology set. Finally, I would like to thank my wife and daughter, to whom this book is dedicated, for the support and encouragement that all writers need and are eternally grateful for.

INTRODUCTION

Life began in the oceans of ancient Earth more than 3 billion years ago. At that time, our planet was a wild and stormy place with an atmosphere that was not fit to breathe. Although the storms were violent, life could not have appeared without them. The lightning provided the energy to make certain molecules that all living things need, and the wind churned up the surface of the soupy seas like a diligent cook stirring a pot. The storms had to stir that pot for a billion years before it finally happened: a tiny bubble, too small to see with the naked eye, gave birth to the first cell, and in the wink of a cosmic eye, the earth was teeming with life.

The first cells were little more than microscopic bags of chemicals that were capable of reproduction. They lived solitary lives but eventually, after learning how to communicate with each other, began to form small colonies consisting of no more than three or four cells each. As time passed, cell-to-cell communication and cooperation became so elaborate that the first simple colonies were transformed into complex multicellular plants and animals. The first cell colonies were produced almost 3 billion years ago by prokaryotes, a simple kind of cell more commonly known as bacteria. Supercells called eukaryotes, appearing about 2 billion years ago, created much more elaborate colonies that eventually gave rise to true multicellular organisms. Eukaryotes are the direct descendants of the prokaryotes, but they are larger, more complex, and more adept at cell-to-cell communication. Plants and animals are all made from eukaryotes. The human body, for example, is made from more than 100 billion eukaryotes, a population consisting of more than 200 different cell types that are organized into organs and tissues. Our brains alone are constructed from 10 billion eukaryotes called neurons that are linked together in a network of enormous complexity. Some neurons in our brain are capable of communicating simultaneously with 100,000 other neurons. It is this level of complexity that pro-duces our intellect and gives us the powers of speech and vision. In some sense, the human brain is the ultimate colony, the most intricate cellular community ever to appear on Earth.

Our understanding of the cell has increased tremendously since the 1970s, when recombinant DNA technology was first introduced. This technology made it possible to study the structure and function of a cell in minute detail. Prior to the 1970s, biologists had only a basic understanding of the cell; they knew the DNA was located in the nucleus, that the cell was surrounded by what appeared to be a feature-less membrane, and that the cell interior was full of structures called organelles, but their functions were largely unknown. Today scientists have sequenced the entire human genome, as well as the genomes of many other organisms. They have determined the function of virtually every cellular organelle, and they have shown that the cell membrane, far from being featureless, contains a molecular forest that gives the cell its eyes, its ears, and the equipment it needs to capture food and to communicate with other cells.

By studying the cell, we improve our understanding of the living world and, in particular, our understanding of plant and animal physiology, genetics, and biochemistry. This wealth of information has revolutionized the biological and medical sciences. For human society, this knowledge translates into a dramatic reduction in mortalities due to infectious diseases and medical disorders. The war on cancer, begun more than 20 years ago, is finally approaching a stage where all cancers will be curable. Improved treatment and prognosis is now possible for many other disorders, such as cardiovascular disease, diabetes, and cystic fibrosis. Improved knowledge of the cell made it possible for researchers to isolate and culture stem cells, a very resourceful kind of cell that may be used to treat spinal cord trauma and degenerative neuro-logical diseases such as Alzheimer's disease and Parkinson's disease. In 1996, scientists in Scotland, using newly acquired knowledge about the way cells divide, performed the most dramatic biological experiment ever conducted when they cloned a sheep named Dolly. Far from being a clever trick, this accomplishment may provide the world with a ready source of therapeutic drugs that could save millions of human lives each year.

This book, the first in the New Biology series, covers the structure and function of the cell with a special emphasis on cell division and cell-to-cell communication (also known as cell signaling). The cell's ability to communicate was essential for the development of multicellular creatures. Moreover, the corruption of that ability, and the process of cell division, is central to many pathological conditions such as cancer and Alzheimer's disease. The corruption of cell signaling and cell division are also responsible for many of the changes that occur in animals as they grow old. The first three chapters of this book discuss the origin of life, the emergence of prokaryotes, and the appearance of eukaryotes. Eukaryotes are the main subject of the book. Subsequent chapters are devoted to discussions of the cell cycle, genes and genetic mechanisms, and the transition, initiated by eukaryotes, from single cells to multicellular organisms. One chapter is devoted to the neuron, an especially talented eukaryote that made the transition to multicellular creatures a possibility. The final chapter provides background material on recombinant DNA technology and other topics that are relevant to cell biology.

.1.

THE ORIGIN OF LIFE

Life began so long ago that many people believe it is impossible to reconstruct the events that led to the appearance of the first cell. The skepticism is understandable, since there are no fossils from that period to study and our knowledge of the Earth's formative years is still rudimentary. Nevertheless, some progress has been made by studying the most primitive cells on Earth today and by conducting laboratory experiments that attempt to reconstruct, in a test tube, the conditions of ancient Earth.

The Big Bang

Fifteen billion years ago, everything in the universe was a soupy concoction of plasma compressed into an area smaller than the head of a pin. There was no matter as we think of it now: no iron, no copper, no carbon, and no oxygen. Just subatomic particles brought together by a crushing force of gravity. No one knows how long the universe remained in this state or even if time, as we know it, existed. We do know that it was extremely hot, with temperatures exceeding 10 billion degrees, 1,000 times hotter than the center of the Sun. Eventually, something happened (no one knows what), and that pinhead of unimaginable heat and density suddenly exploded. Within seconds, the temperature dropped enough for atomic nuclei to form; after a million years, the temperature was low enough for the first elements to appear. The first of these was hydrogen, the simplest of all elements, and the one that gave rise to all the rest. Although the universe was cooling down, it was still hot enough to fuse hydrogen atoms to produce helium. Enough hydrogen and helium were formed in this way to produce all the stars and galaxies. Heat within the stars was sufficient to fuse hydrogen and helium atoms to form all the other elements that we now find in nature, such as carbon, iron, copper, and nitrogen.

The Importance of Violent Storms

Ten billion years after the big bang, our Earth was created as a molten ball of metal and stone thrown off by the sun during the formation of the solar system. Additional material was added to our planet as it collided with asteroids and meteors. The high surface temperature liberated an enormous amount of water vapor from the nearly molten rocks. The vapor rose into the atmosphere, forming a heavy cloud layer that completely enshrouded the planet, effectively blocking the sun's rays. During the subsequent half-billion years, the Earth cooled down, and when it did, the rains began to fall. This was no brief summer shower, but a pelting rain that lasted hundreds of years and led to the formation of the oceans, which covered most of the Earth's surface just as they do

An artist's conception of prebiotic Earth showing a volcano and the hot, stormy environment. (*Courtesy of Steve Munsinger/Photo Researchers, Inc.*)

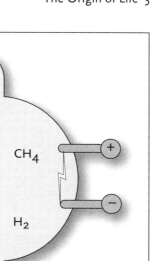

Urey-Miller experiment to simulate conditions on prebiotic Earth. Water is heated in a closed system containing methane (CH_4), ammonia (NH_3), and hydrogen (H_2) gases. An electric discharge is passed through the vaporized mixture to simulate lightning in the atmosphere. Synthesized compounds collect in the trap and are sampled by opening the spigot. The original experiment was run for a week or more before samples were collected.

today. The land was barren and wracked with volcanic eruptions that spewed noxious gases such as methane (CH_4) and ammonia (NH_3) into the atmosphere. The air contained very little, if any, free oxygen.

A planet with an atmosphere of methane and ammonia does not, at first glance, appear a likely candidate for the origin of life. Modern cells need oxygen to breathe and require four kinds of organic molecules: amino acids (building blocks for proteins), nucleic acids (building blocks for DNA and RNA), fats, and sugars. This is a short list, but a long way from methane and ammonia. Nevertheless, in 1953, Harold Urey, a professor at the University of Chicago, and his gradate student, Stanley Miller, decided to test the hypothesis that Earth's ancient atmosphere, combined with fierce electric storms, was essential for the production of the molecules that cells need to live.

To conduct the experiment, Miller constructed a simple test-tube apparatus consisting of two round flasks connected by glass tubing. One of the flasks, containing water, simulated the ocean; a second flask, filled with hydrogen, methane, and ammonia gases, served as the atmosphere. They passed an electric discharge through the flask containing the atmosphere to simulate lightning and heated the water flask to produce the high temperature of the young earth. After a week, Urey and Miller tested the contents of the flask and to their great surprise found that the water contained large amounts of amino acids. By varying the conditions of their experiment they were able to produce a wide variety of organic compounds, including nucleic acids, sugars, and fats.

Essential Molecules Formed Spontaneously

The Urey-Miller experiment made it clear that the basic building blocks for life could have been made in the harsh, prebiotic (before life) Earth environment. Given the conditions of that period, it now seems almost inevitable that such molecules would be synthesized. These results, published in 1953, generated a great deal of excitement, both in the science community and among the general public. Many people believed we were close to understanding the origin of life itself, a feat that had seemed impossible just a few years earlier. The Urey-Miller experiment suggested that the conditions on earth 4.5 billion years ago led to the formation of certain key organic molecules, which assembled themselves into larger molecules that eventually went on to form the first cell. However, much of the optimism that this experiment generated began to fade under the cloud of an impenetrable paradox.

Modern cells depend heavily on an interaction between proteins and nucleic acids (DNA and RNA). The proteins are used to construct the cell, and a special group of them, called enzymes, control the many chemical reactions that are necessary for cells to live. DNA is a collection of blueprints, or genes, that store the information to make the proteins. One kind of RNA, called messenger RNA (mRNA), serves as an intermediary between the genes and the cell's machinery for synthesizing proteins. Although it is possible for nucleic acids and proteins to self-assemble, it is extremely unlikely that the modern relationship between the three developed spontaneously. It comes down to the age-old question of which came first, the chicken or the egg: the nucleic acids or the proteins? Could DNA, or RNA, have self-assembled and then orchestrated the synthesis of the proteins? Or did the proteins self-assemble and then make their own blueprints using DNA, while ignoring RNA altogether? Before we attempt to resolve this paradox, we must consider in a little more detail the kinds of molecules that cells need to survive.

Modern cells are biochemical entities that synthesize many thousands of molecules. Studying these chemicals, and the biochemistry of the cell, would be a daunting task were it not for the fact that most of the chemical variation is based on six types of molecules that are assembled into just four types of macromolecules. The six basic molecules are amino acids, phosphate, glycerol, sugars, fatty acids, and nucleotides. Amino acids have a simple core structure consisting of an amino group, a carboxyl group, and a variable R group attached to a carbon atom. There are 20 different kinds of amino acids, each with a unique R group. Phosphates are extremely important molecules that are used in the construction, or modification, of many other molecules. They are also used to store chemical-bond energy. Glycerol is a simple three-carbon alcohol that is an important component of cell membranes and fat reservoirs. Sugars are extremely versatile molecules that are used as an energy source and for structural purposes. Glucose, a six-carbon sugar, is the primary energy source for most cells, and it is the principle sugar used to glycosylate proteins and lipids that form the outer coat of all cells. Plants have exploited the structural potential of sugars in their production of cellulose, and thus wood, bark, grasses, and reeds are polymers of glucose and other monosaccharides. Ribose, a five-carbon sugar, is a component of nucleic acids, as well as the cell's main energy depot, adenosine triphosphate (ATP). The numbering convention for sugar carbon atoms is shown in the accompanying

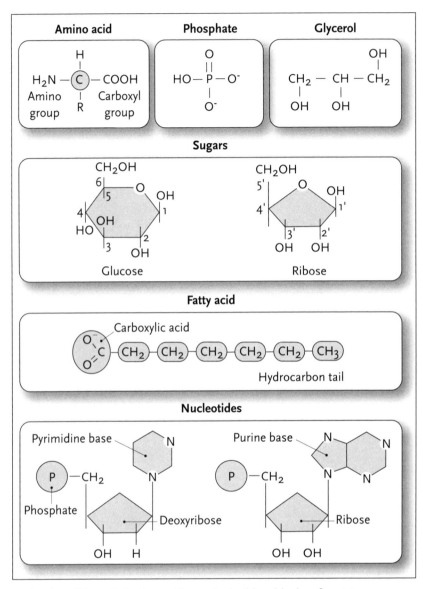

Molecules of the cell. Amino acids are the building blocks of proteins. Phosphate is an important component of many other molecules and is added to proteins to modify their behavior. Glycerol is a three-carbon alcohol that is an important ingredient in cell membranes and fat. Sugars, like glucose, are a primary energy source for most cells and also have many structural functions. Fatty acids are involved in the production of cell membranes and storage of fat. Nucleotides are the building blocks for DNA and RNA.

figure. Ribose carbons are numbered as 1' (1 prime), 2', and so on. Consequently, references to nucleic acids, which include ribose, often refer to the 3' or 5' carbon. Fatty acids consist of a carboxyl group (when ionized it becomes a carboxylic acid) linked to a hydrophobic hydrocarbon tail. These molecules are used in the construction of cell membranes and fat. Nucleotides are building blocks for DNA (deoxyribonucleic acid) and RNA (ribonucleic acid). Nucleotides consist of three components: a phosphate, a ribose sugar, and a nitrogenous (nitrogen containing) ring compound that behaves as a base in solution. Nucleotide bases appear in two forms: a single-ring nitrogenous base, called a pyrimidine, and a double-ringed base, called a purine. There are two kinds of purines (adenine and guanine), and three pyramidines (uracil, cytosine, and thymine). Uracil is specific to RNA, substituting for thymine. In addition, RNA nucleotides contain ribose, whereas DNA nucleotides contain deoxyribose (hence the origin of their names). Ribose has a hydroxyl (OH) group attached to both the 2' and 3' carbons, whereas deoxyribose is missing the 2' hydroxyl group.

The six basic molecules are used by all cells to construct five essential macromolecules. These include proteins, RNA, DNA, phospholipids, and sugar polymers, known as polysaccharides. Amino acids are linked together by peptide bonds to construct a protein. A peptide bond is formed by linking the carboxyl end of one amino acid to the amino end of a second amino acid. Thus, once constructed, every protein has an amino end, and a carboxyl end. An average protein may consist of 300 to 400 amino acids. Nucleic acids are macromolecules constructed from nucleotides. RNA nucleotides are adenine, uracil, cytosine, and guanine. This nucleic acid is generally single-stranded but can form localized double-stranded regions. RNA is involved in the synthesis of proteins and is a structural and enzymatic component of ribosomes. DNA, a double-stranded nucleic acid, encodes cellular genes and is constructed from adenine, thymine, cytosine, and guanine deoxyribonucleotides (hence, the name deoxyribonucleic acid). The two DNA strands coil around each other like strands in a piece of rope, and for this reason the molecule is known as the double helix. Phospholipids, the main component in cell membranes, are composed of a polar head group (usually an alcohol), a phosphate, glycerol, and two hydrophobic fatty acid tails. Fat that is stored in the body as an energy reserve has a structure similar to

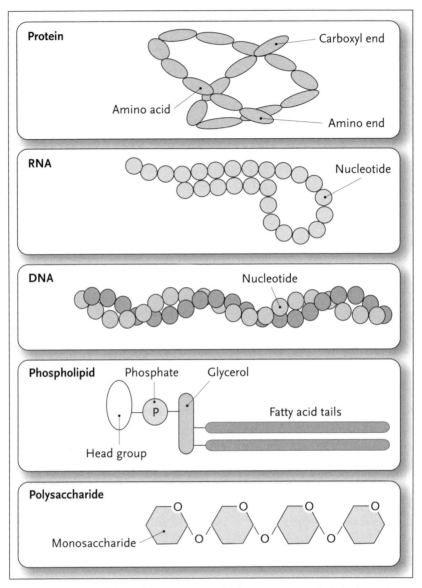

Macromolecules of the cell. Protein is made from amino acids linked together to form a long chain that can fold up into a three-dimensional structure. RNA and DNA are long chains of nucleotides. RNA is generally single-stranded but can form localized double-stranded regions. DNA is a double-stranded helix, with one strand coiling around the other. A phospholipid is composed of a hydrophilic head-group, a phosphate, a glycerol molecule, and two hydrophobic fatty acid tails. Polysaccharides are sugar polymers.

a phospholipid, being composed of three fatty acid chains attached to a molecule of glycerol. The third fatty acid takes the place of the phosphate and head group of a phospholipid. Sugars are polymerized to form chains of two or more monosaccharides. Disaccharides (two monosaccharides), and oligosaccharides (about 3–12 monosaccharides), are attached to proteins and lipids destined for the cell surface. Polysaccharides, such as glycogen and starch, may contain several hundred monosaccharides and are stored in cells as an energy reserve.

All the molecules shown in the accompanying figure are assumed to have formed in the prebiotic oceans, and this was followed by auto-assembly of the macromolecules. Auto-assembly of the nucleic acids could have produced polymers that were 60–100 nucleotides long. With one DNA or RNA strand made, a second strand would have formed automatically through base pairing; that is, the formation of chemical bonds between the nitrogenous bases. The chemistry of these bases is such that cytosine always pairs with guanine, while adenine always pairs with thymine. In the case of RNA, which lacks thymine, adenine pairs with uracil. Thus, pairing is always between a purine and a pyrimidine, and the association between the two can form spontaneously. Base pairing, also known as hybridization, can form between two DNA molecules or between a DNA and an RNA molecule. Self-hybridization, involving a single DNA or RNA molecule, can also occur. Because the early oceans were hot, double-stranded DNA or RNA came apart through dissociation of the two chains. That is, the prevailing heat broke (or melted) the chemical bonds holding each nucleotide pair together without disrupting the two chains or strands. When the strands separate, the cycle repeats with another round of base pairing leading to the production of two more double-stranded molecules, one of which contains the original strand and the other contains its exact copy.

By exploiting the properties of nucleotide base-pairing, coupled with the high temperatures of primitive Earth, short pieces of DNA and RNA can replicate without the aid of any other molecules. In modern cells, DNA remains double-stranded, and in prebiotic earth, with much higher temperatures than we have today, it may still have been slower to dissociate than RNA. Thus RNA replication would have proceeded much more quickly, producing a larger, more diverse population of molecules.

Life Began in an RNA World

The molecule that led to the first living cell would have to be able to replicate itself as well as function as an enzyme. DNA fulfills the first condition, but it has no known enzymatic activity, and at the time of the Urey-Miller experiment, this was thought to be the case for RNA as well: Both were believed to be incapable of regulating chemical reactions, so that neither could build protein molecules by themselves. Pro-

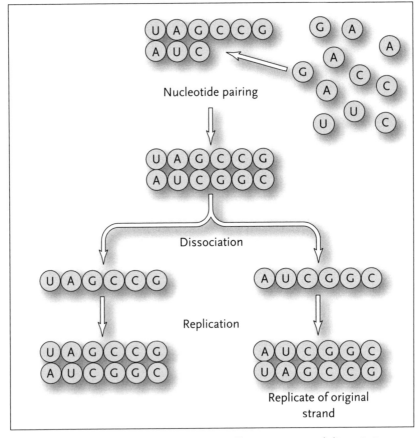

Self-replication of RNA through a process of base pairing and dissociation. Soon after replication, the two double strands separate into four single-stranded molecules, one of which is identical to the original strand. DNA can self-replicate through the same mechanisms.

teins, on the other hand, make efficient enzymes but cannot replicate themselves. This paradox was about to bring an end to origin-of-life studies when, in 1983, Thomas Cech at the University of Colorado, and Sidney Altman at Yale University discovered the ribozyme, an RNA molecule capable of enzymatic activity. This discovery led almost immediately to the suggestion that the first cells came to life in an RNA world.

Ribozymes, assembled in the prebiotic oceans, could not only replicate themselves but also could have catalyzed the formation of specific proteins, which in turn could have functioned as structural proteins or enzymes. Eventually, a protein enzyme appeared that could copy RNA into DNA (such an enzyme, called reverse transcriptase, does exist), and when that happened, the cell's machinery approached a modern level of organization: DNA serving as the blueprint, and RNA acting as an intermediary in the process of protein synthesis. Shifting to a DNA-based genome meant that cells could become much more complex because DNA, as a double-stranded molecule, is more stable than RNA and thus capable of storing information for many more genes.

Once upon a Wave

The concept of the RNA world is very compelling, yet in itself it cannot explain the appearance of the first cell. The auto-assembly of ribozymes and proteins is of little use if they are not confined in some way. But how was this to happen? Organic molecules, newly synthesized by the raging storms, were swept along and dispersed by the wind and currents. If a ribozyme appeared that could make an especially useful protein, the association between the two would have been quickly lost. However, winds sweeping across the ocean have a way of driving things onto shore, so it is possible that organic molecules collected, and were concentrated, along the seashore much like driftwood collecting on a beach. The water near the shore, being shallower than in the open oceans, would also tend to be warmer, concentrating the organic molecules even further through evaporation. Shorelines have another important property that is of interest here. Anyone who has stood on a beach and watched a wave break has witnessed one of the most important mechanisms for the formation of life on this planet:

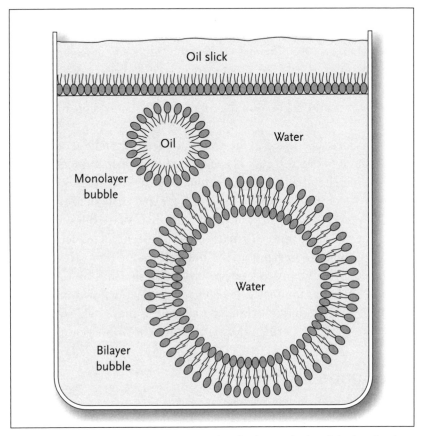

Phospholipid bubbles. Phospholipid molecules have a hydrophilic headend (shaded ovals) and two hydrophobic tails that do not mix with water and will avoid being surrounded by it. In an oil slick, the hydrophobic tails mix with the oil while the heads stay close to the water. In turbulence, phospholipids form two kinds of bubbles: a monolayer that can only capture a drop of oil and a bilayer that can capture a drop of water. The bilayer allows the hydrophobic tails to associate with themselves, while the heads associate with water on both the inside and outside surfaces of the bubble.

The foam that rolls into shore after the wave breaks is composed of billions of bubbles.

In the prebiotic coastal waters, each bubble that formed collected a different sample of the water and, therefore, represented a unique individual, a separate experiment that could be acted upon by the forces of natural selection. But as we stand on a beach watching the waves break on the shore, we notice that the foam in the surf disappears very quickly. There is nothing to hold the bubbles together; that is, unless there happens to be a layer of oil on the surface of the water. Bubbles made from oil tend to have a much longer life span. Coincidentally, among the organic molecules synthesized in the prebiotic oceans was the oily compound phospholipid. These molecules may be drawn as a bead, representing the hydrophilic head group, linked to the hydrophobic fatty acid tails. Phospholipids have the unusual property of being hydrophilic (able to mix with water) at the beaded end, but hydrophobic (unable to mix with water) at the tail end. This is curious behavior, but extremely important for the origin of life. Biologists believe that phospholipids were produced by the storms of ancient earth, forming Earth's first oil slick very close to shore, in relatively calm bays and lagoons. Stir up the water with a driving wind and rolling surf, and the phospholipids will produce billions of tiny, stable bubbles.

Phospholipids have another curious, but very important, property: They can form bubbles out of a monolayer (single layer) of molecules or they can form bubbles out of a bilayer (two layers) of molecules. In a monolayer, the external surface of the bubble is always the hydrophilic end of the molecule, whereas the inside of the bubble contains the hydrophobic portion. This type of bubble can only trap oils, not water, and therefore could never lead to the production of a cell. On the other hand, a bubble formed from a bilayer has a hydrophilic surface on both the exterior and interior surfaces. Such a bubble can trap water and water-soluble molecules like ribozymes, sugars, and proteins.

The lipid bilayer is a humble structure, and at first glance may seem as though it is of little consequence, but life could not have arisen without it. Lipid-bilayer bubbles, forming in the seas of ancient Earth, could remain intact long enough to experiment with the molecules and macromolecules they captured when they were formed. If a bubble happened to pick up, or assemble, a protein that stabilized the walls of the bubble, then that bubble had an advantage over the others and would have extra time to experiment with the synthesis of novel ribozymes and proteins. We can imagine this process leading to a primitive form of genetic inheritance. When the bubbles burst, they released the results of their experiments into the water. When new bubbles formed, they may have captured some, or all, of those molecules and thus have been given a head start through the inheritance of a simple gene pool. This process, acted upon by natural selection, is believed to have transformed the prebiotic bubbles into the first cells.

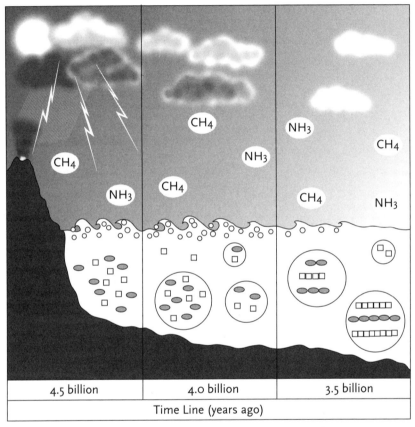

4.5 billion	4.0 billion	3.5 billion
	Time Line (years ago)	

The origin of the first cells. Organic molecules essential for life were synthesized spontaneously 4.5 billion years ago when Earth was hot, stormy, and wracked with constant volcanic eruptions. Some of the organic molecules were captured by lipid bubbles (white circles) formed by ocean turbulence near a shoreline, and by 3.5 million years ago the first cells learned how to assemble the molecules into a variety of polymers. Nucleic acids, amino acids, fats, and sugars were among the organic molecules produced in the prebiotic oceans; only the nucleic acids (white squares) and amino acids (gray ovals) are shown. Major gases in the atmosphere included methane (CH_4) and ammonia (NH_3).

Modern cells all have a membrane constructed from a phospholipid bilayer. From the very beginning, cells used the lipid bilayer to regulate their internal environment. The bilayer blocked, or impeded, the passive flow of most molecules into the cell, thus protecting the cell from the external environment. Cells exploited this property by embedding proteins in their membranes that would allow only certain molecules to gain entry. In this way, the cell could fine-tune the selection of what got in and what did not. Other proteins embedded in the membrane acted like sensory antennae, making it possible for cells to gain information about their immediate environment. Some of these proteins were used to detect the presence of food molecules, while others became specialized as transmitters and receivers, allowing the cells to communicate with each other. Cell-to-cell communication led to the next stage in the development of life on our planet. Single cells began to form colonies of increasing complexity, eventually transforming themselves into the multicellular creatures that now inhabit the Earth.

The Classification of Cells

The first cells, appearing 3.5 billion years ago, quickly evolved into ancestral prokaryotes and, about 2 billion years ago, gave rise to Archaea, bacteria, and eukaryotes, the three major divisions of life in the world. Eukaryotes, in turn, gave rise to plants, animals, protozoans, and fungi. Each of these groups represents a distinct phylogenetic kingdom. The Archaea and bacteria represent a fifth kingdom, known as the Monera, or prokaryotes. The Archaea are prokaryotes that are physically similar to bacteria (both lack a nucleus and internal organelles), but they have retained a primitive biochemistry and physiology that would have been commonplace 2 billion years ago. Most Archaea are anaerobic and can live in extreme conditions of high temperature (sometimes hot enough to cook an egg) and high salt concentrations. All these conditions were common on Earth 3 billion years ago and make the Archaea seem like living fossils. For the Archaea, oxygen is a toxic substance, and for this reason they are always found living underground, or in deep thermal vents where the concentration of oxygen is very low. There are some bacteria that are also anaerobic but they can tolerate higher concentrations of oxygen than can the Archaea. Eukaryotes

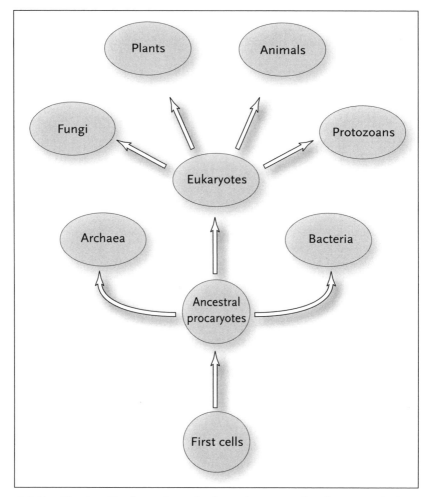

Cell Classification. The first cells evolved into the ancestral prokaryotes, which gave rise to the Archaea, bacteria, and eukaryotes, the three major divisions of life in the world. The Archaea and bacteria are very similar anatomically but differ biochemically. Eukaryotes, anatomically and biochemically distinct from both the Archaea and bacteria, gave rise to plants, animals, protozoans, and fungi.

(meaning "true nucleus") are much more complex than the prokaryotes, having many membrane-bounded organelles and a large genome. These cells are the primary focus of this book and the other volumes in this set.

.2.

PROKARYOTES
Laying the Foundations

The first cells appeared on earth more than 3 billion years ago and quickly evolved into prokaryotes, more commonly known as bacteria. For more than a billion years, prokaryotes were the only things alive on the face of the Earth. During those billion years, bacteria were likely confined to tide pools and shallow seas, but eventually they came to inhabit virtually every niche available in the water, on the land, and in the air.

A Simple but Versatile Cell

All bacteria are extremely small and invisible to the naked eye. Over a thousand of these cells would fit within a period on this page. No one knew that bacteria, or any other cell, existed until a Dutch lens grinder named Antonie van Leeuwenhoek made the first high-resolution microscope in 1660. Leeuwenhoek's microscope consisted of a single lens mounted in a small brass frame, to which he attached a slender arm for holding a specimen. One September evening in 1683, he looked at a sample of dental plaque taken from his own teeth and the next morning wrote an excited letter to the Royal Society of London describing the many "animalcules" that he had discovered.

Two hundred years later, microscopes and the field of biology had developed to such an extent that more than 1,500 bacterial species had been discovered and described in detail (as described in chapter 8). This wealth of information not only set the stage for the new biology that was to come but gave us the theoretical framework to understand many diseases that had plagued humankind since the origin of our species.

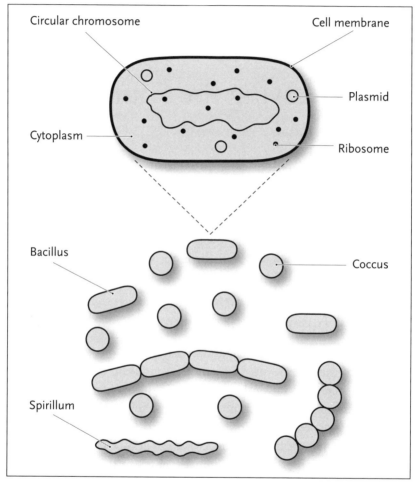

Prokaryotes. All prokaryotes have the same basic anatomy consisting of a cell membrane, cytoplasm and a circular DNA chromosome. Some bacteria have a second, smaller chromosome called a plasmid, which may be present in multiple copies. The cytoplasm contains a wide assortment of enzymes and molecules, as well as ribosomes, protein-RNA complexes that are involved in protein synthesis. The cells may be spherical (coccus), rod shaped (bacillus), or wavy corkscrews (spirillum), appearing singly, in pairs, or linked together into short chains.

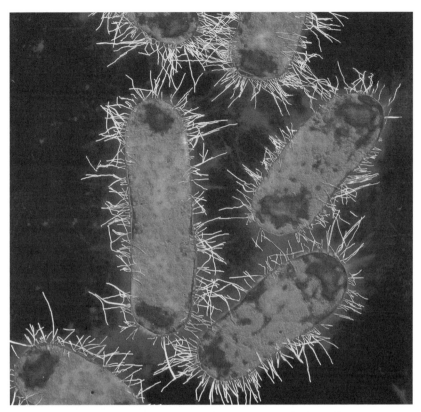

Scanning electron micrograph (SEM) of the rod-shaped ciliated bacteria *Eschericia coli,* commonly known as *E. coli.* These bacteria are a normal part of the intestinal flora but certain strains may cause gastroenteritis. *E. coli* is also commonly used in genetic studies. Magnification: 25,000x. *(Courtesy of Eye of Science/Photo Researchers, Inc.)*

All bacteria have the same simple anatomy, consisting primarily of three parts: a cell membrane, protoplasm (or cytoplasm), and a chromosome. The cell membrane, often surrounded by a cell wall, is a phospholipid bilayer, identical in kind to that which formed around the prebiotic bubbles. The cytoplasm is an aqueous gel that contains a wide assortment of enzymes and molecules, and millions of spherical bodies called ribosomes that are involved in protein synthesis. Prokaryote ribosomes are complex structures consisting of more than 50 different proteins and three RNA molecules. Although the proteins

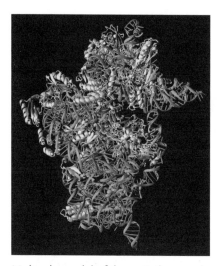

Molecule model of the 30S ribosomal subunit, which consists of protein (light gray corkscrew structures) and RNA (coiled ladders). The overall shape of the molecule is determined by the RNA, which is also responsible for the catalytic function of the ribosome. *(Courtesy of V. Ramakrishnan, MRC Laboratory of Molecular Biology, Cambridge)*

outnumber the RNA, two-thirds of the ribosome's mass is due to the RNA. Before ribozymes were discovered, it was assumed the proteins existed in the ribosome as enzymes. We now know, however, that the RNA molecules catalyze the formation of new proteins, while the ribosomal proteins serve a structural role, perhaps acting as a scaffold to hold the amino acids in position before they are linked together.

The bacterial cytoplasm also contains the cell's chromosome: a single circular piece of DNA that holds all the genes, collectively referred to as the genome. Molecular biologists, using recombinant DNA technology (described in chapter 8), have found that a typical prokaryote has 2,000 to 4,000 genes, with each gene coding for a single protein. Many bacteria have a second, smaller chromosome called a plasmid. Like the main chromosome, the plasmid is circular, but it carries only two or three genes. Plasmid genes have been sequenced and are known to code for proteins that can neutralize antibiotics, such as penicillin or streptomycin. Placing antibiotic-resistant genes on an auxiliary chromosome is a brilliant maneuver. The cell can only have one copy of the main chromosome, but it can have many copies of the plasmid. Consequently, bacteria that have plasmids can produce a large amount of antibiotic-resistant proteins in a very short time. Plasmids make the control of pathogenic bacteria very difficult, but as we will see, their existence was crucial for the development of the new biology.

Because bacteria have such a simple structure, it is often impossible, even under a high-powered microscope, to tell one species from another. In a few cases, there are clear structural differences: Some bacteria are spherical, whereas others are shaped like short rods. Both types of bacteria can appear singly or linked together into chains of varying lengths. Many rod-shaped bacteria are covered with hairlike cilia or have a single tail-like flagellum to propel the cell through the water. This type of bacterium is said to be motile. Biologists have measured the speed of these cells and have found that if they were the size of a rowboat, they could travel through the water at 60 miles per hour. Spherical bacteria are never ciliated and therefore cannot propel themselves through the water. This type of bacterium is said to be non-motile.

Despite the simple morphology of prokaryotes, their physiology and biochemistry are surprisingly complex. The Earth environment, whether in water, soil, or air, contains an enormous variety of organic molecules, and for each molecule there is a bacterium that is able to use it as a source of food.

The Quest for Power

When we strike a match to wood in our fireplace, we gather to enjoy the warmth of the fire, produced by the release of energy stored in the molecular structure of the wood. By striking the match, we are triggering a chain reaction that liberates the energy in one roaring step. In their quest for power, cells learned to avoid roaring steps because they generate so much heat that most of the energy is lost.

Acquiring energy is one of the most important problems that prokaryotes had to solve. The first cells lived in an ocean filled with small molecules, produced in the prebiotic environment. Each of these molecules was like a small piece of wood that the cell could use as a source of energy. The trick was to extract the energy very carefully so as not to lose most of it in a burst of heat and light. Extracting energy in this way is the job of an enzyme. Enzymes can pick a molecule apart piece by piece, supplying small amounts of energy at each stage. The energy so released can be used directly to perform a task, or it can be stored for later use. Extracting energy by breaking a molecule down is called catabolism. Anabolism is just the reverse; it uses energy to build molecules. Cellular metabolism is the combination of catabolic and anabolic activity.

Of all the molecules created in the prebiotic oceans, glucose was the most important as a source of food. Cells prefer glucose to this day, and for some, like the neurons in our brain, it is the only molecule they will

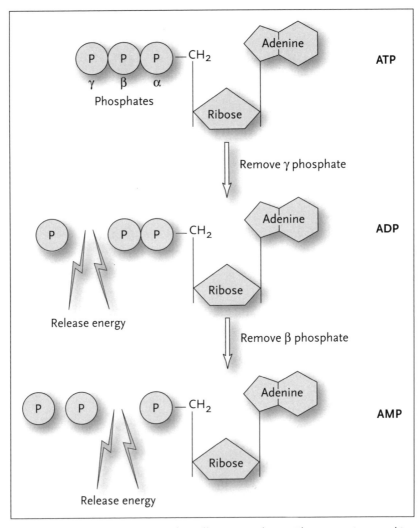

Adenosine triphosphate (ATP), the cell's energy depot. The energy is stored in the covalent bonds linking the phosphates together. Breaking the gamma (γ) phosphate bond releases energy, converting ATP to adenosine diphosphate (ADP). Additional energy may be released by breaking the beta (β) bond, converting ADP to adenosine monophosphate (AMP). AMP is converted back to ATP by mitochondria.

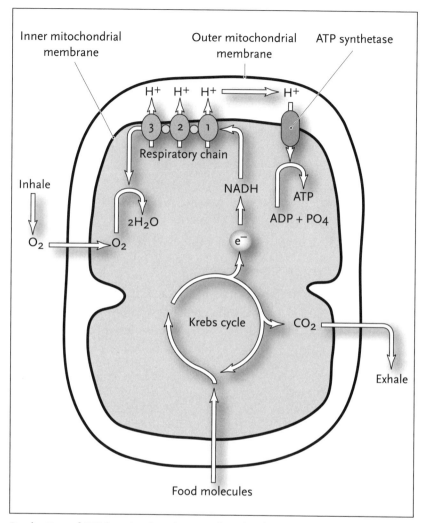

Production of ATP by mitochondria. Food molecules are processed through the Krebs cycle to produce electrons (e⁻) that are stored in NADH. The respiratory chain consists of three major components: NADH dehydrogenase (1), cytochrome b (2), and cytochrome oxidase (3). The first component in the chain captures the stored electrons by separating NADH into NAD and H⁺ (not shown). The electrons travel through the chain powering a pumping function of each component resulting in a proton (H⁺) concentration gradient across the inner membrane and are eventually transferred to oxygen (O_2), leading to the production of water. The protons, moving down their concentration gradient, power the synthesis of ATP by the synthetase. The only exhaust from this power plant is water, which the cell uses, and CO_2, a gas that is exhaled by the lungs.

use. Prokaryotes can use glucose directly or, in some cases, send it through an anabolic pathway to form a polymer called glycogen (a long chain of glucose molecules), which can be stored in the cell for later use.

Prokaryotes also developed a method for storing some of the energy that is released when glucose is broken down. This procedure is called glycolysis, a very ancient catabolic pathway that produces two molecules of ATP for every molecule of glucose that is broken down. ATP stores energy in phosphate bonds, and this energy is released when these bonds are broken. If an enzyme requires energy for a job that it has to do, it can either break (or hydrolyze) a phosphate bond on ATP, or, if it lacks that ability, the cell recruits another enzyme that has ATPase activity (that is, the enzyme is able to hydrolyze the phosphate bond). Prokaryotes often recruit many enzymes to perform a given task. The complete catabolism of a molecule of glucose by the glycolytic pathway requires 10 different enzymes. Because it does not require oxygen, it is referred to as an anaerobic metabolic pathway.

A half-million years after the first prokaryotes appeared, some of them learned to build organic molecules by using energy collected from the sun. A by-product of this photosynthetic pathway is the release of oxygen. Eventually, other cells, unable to perform photosynthesis, learned to use the oxygen to extract energy from an even wider variety of molecules than was possible with glycolysis. Two aerobic (requiring oxygen) metabolic pathways were developed; one of these is called the citric acid cycle (or the Krebs cycle, after the biochemist who discovered it), and the other is called the electron transport chain (also called the respiratory chain). These two pathways work in tandem to extract energy from fats, simple sugars, polysaccharides, and amino acids.

Unlike glycolysis, the Krebs cycle stores most of the energy that it liberates in electrons, which are carried by special molecules through the respiratory chain where their energy is used to make ATP. The by-products of these two pathways are water and carbon dioxide (CO_2). The coordinated activity of the Krebs cycle and the respiratory chain is analogous to the way we generate electricity to run our factories and to make our homes comfortable. A power generator, usually at a hydroelectric dam, plays the role of the citric acid cycle, and the copper wires that carry the current are analogous to the respiratory chain. We use the electricity our power plants produce to turn on lights, heaters, and motors. The cell uses the electricity that it generates for one thing: to make ATP.

Glycolysis, the Krebs cycle, and the respiratory chain are all run and assembled by protein enzymes. These metabolic pathways are used by all prokaryotes that are alive today. The glycolytic pathway and the Krebs cycle are located in the protoplasm, while the respiratory chain is located in the cell membrane. Additional proteins necessary for collecting glucose and other sugars are also located in the cell membrane. These proteins, called glucose transporters or carriers, are specially designed for bringing glucose into the cell. Glucose and other simple sugars can diffuse passively across the cell membrane, but it is a much slower process. Transporters provide a channel that allows the cell to take up glucose 100 times faster than by simple diffusion.

The ability to make glucose carriers that are embedded in the cell membrane was probably the most important event leading to the transition from the first cells to the ancestral prokaryotes. Once cells learned this trick, they expanded on it very quickly. Proteins were embedded in the membrane that could detect and import other sugars, such as maltose or lactose. They even learned how to make sugar receptors, also embedded in the membrane, which could signal the cell when a high concentration of glucose or maltose was encountered so the activity of the transporters could be stepped up accordingly. The electron transport chain may have evolved from proteins that were originally embedded in the membrane to process or detect sugar molecules.

The sugar carriers, receptors, and components of the respiratory chain are all glycoproteins; that is, sugar molecules are attached to the proteins to enhance or modulate their behavior. Glycoproteins are like molecular trees, with the protein portion being the trunk and the sugar molecules forming the leaves and branches. It is almost as though the prokaryotes were building a forest with which to cover themselves, much in the way higher plants covered the surface of the Earth so many millions of years later. The molecular forest of a prokaryote is called the glycocalyx, and its importance to the cell cannot be overstated. This forest gives the cell its eyes, ears, and a sense of touch in addition to the energy-processing machinery. It is through the glycocalyx that cells

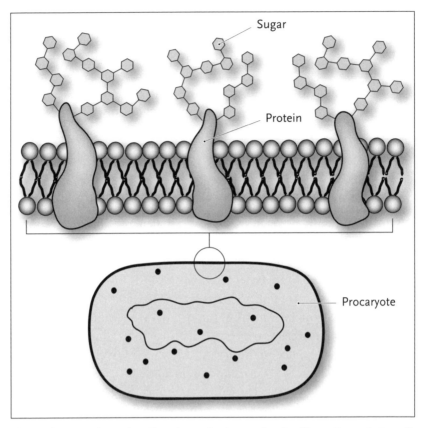

The prokaryote glycocalyx. The glycocalyx is a molecular "forest" consisting of glycoproteins, which covers the outer surface of the cell membrane. In this forest, the "tree trunks" are protein, the "leaves" are sugar molecules, and the "branches" are chemical bonds. Glycoproteins have many jobs, including the transportation and detection of food molecules.

learned how to communicate with one another, paving the way for the appearance of multicellular creatures like ourselves.

The Importance of Good Housekeeping

Acquiring energy is not the only problem that prokaryotes had to deal with. They also had to keep their house in order and be able to make or repair every part of their structure. This was no small feat. By analogy, if our house is damaged we go to the hardware store to buy the lumber for the repairs; but for a cell there is no such store available. Instead, they have to *make* all the materials needed before they can begin to repair themselves.

Prokaryotes have learned to build and repair themselves with the same molecules that they use for food. As mentioned earlier in this chapter, glucose can be converted into glycogen as a food reserve; after being cross-linked with a few amino acids, it is also used to make the cell wall. Higher plants use a similar trick: Wood is nothing more than an elaborate polymer of glucose. The trees that grow on the Earth and the lumber that is used to build our homes are all sugar compounds.

The prokaryotes use many other molecules both for food and for building materials: Fats can be used as a source of food, or they can be converted to phospholipids and used to repair the cell membrane. Many proteins have enzymatic activity and are kept busy running the cell, but there are also many nonenzymatic proteins, which are synthesized as building materials and used to construct cilia, flagella, microtubules, the cytoskeleton, and all the cellular organelles.

A Lost World

Cells came to life in an RNA world, where RNA functioned both as a molecule for storing genetic information and as an enzyme. But RNA is a relatively small and simple molecule. Like an old-fashioned computer with limited memory, it can store only small amounts of genetic information, and its talents as an enzyme are severely limited. This was no great disadvantage to the first cells, since the molecules they were using as a source of energy were also very simple and did not require enzymes more elaborate than a ribozyme. But that world began to change as the small molecules were used up and replaced with more complex molecules, produced by the cells themselves and liberated into the water when they died. Now the cells were faced with a new problem, a new quest: the extraction of energy and building materials from molecules of increasing complexity.

Cells, always inventive, found a solution. However, there may have been a time when their very survival was in doubt, for it meant they had to change the way they had been doing things for millions of years:

They had to abandon the RNA world in favor of DNA and protein. Protein enzymes, being made from 20 different amino acids, can be much more complex than a ribozyme, and therefore they have a greater chance of being able to catabolize complex molecules. Moreover, as the population of complex food molecules increased, cells were forced to keep pace by coming up with new enzymes to deal with them. RNA could not store the genetic information for all the new protein enzymes that cells needed in order to survive; it is for this reason that DNA came to be the molecule of choice for the storage of genetic information.

A New Genetic Order

In the RNA world, the genetic flow was simple and direct: Ribozymes were both genes and enzymes that could synthesize proteins directly. The prokaryotes, however, changed all that. DNA became the molecule of choice for storing the genes, and RNA was left in control of the protein synthesis machinery. This three-step, unidirectional organization of DNA to RNA to protein is now used by all cells, and has many advantages over the system that it replaced. DNA, being a much longer macromolecule than RNA, can store information for thousands of genes. In addition, because it is a double-stranded molecule, DNA is much more stable than RNA, and the presence of two strands provides a way of repairing the genes if they are ever damaged. That is, because of nucleotide pairing, the damaged strand can be repaired using the complementary strand as a guide.

In the new genetic order, the molecule carrying the gene itself is not being used to synthesize the protein, so there is no chance that it will be damaged during the translation process. There is a real-world analogy to this organization: Human architects and engineers make blueprints to guide them in the production of houses, cars, boats, and many other structures. Those blueprints are always kept in a safe place so nothing will ever happen to them, and the only time they are taken out of the filing cabinet is to make a copy, or a working blueprint, that is given to the carpenters so they can build our new home. The carpenters may spill coffee on it, step on it, or crumple it up if they want to, because they always have the original to refer back to. In the cell, the working blueprint is a molecule called messenger RNA (mRNA), so named because it is, in effect, carrying a genetic message from the chromosome to the ribosomes. Copying a gene into mRNA occurs by a process known as transcription. Once the ribosomes receive the mRNA, the ribosomal RNA (rRNA) molecules use it to synthesize the protein in a process known as translation. From this we can see that while RNA lost its job as a genetic reservoir, it remains in control of protein synthesis.

No one knows how DNA came to be the cell's gene bank, but it is possible the enzymatic proteins orchestrated the change themselves. There is a protein enzyme called reverse transcriptase that can copy RNA into DNA, and the reverse transcription process that it performs may have been the way the DNA genome originally appeared. Moreover, protein enzymes are capable of surprisingly complex behavior, almost as though they are living entities unto themselves. In prokaryotes, and in all modern cells, there are proteins that take care of the DNA much like shepherds tending their flocks. Some of these molecular shepherds constantly scan the DNA for damage and, if they find any, repair it. Several protein enzymes are in charge of replicating DNA in preparation for cell division, and still others are needed to copy a gene into messenger RNA in preparation for protein synthesis.

The interaction between the proteins and the DNA is of mutual benefit and important for the survival of the cell. All proteins have a very short life span, sometimes no more than a day or two, so it is to their advantage to take care of the genes. In a sense, this relationship between DNA and protein is a form of molecular symbiosis, in which both parties benefit. The cell as a whole is the ultimate beneficiary, since a good working relationship between the enzymes and the DNA makes it more adaptable and better able to survive in a changing environment.

In building their new genetic order, the prokaryotes had to develop a method for interpreting the sequence information stored in the DNA molecule. DNA is a linear sequence of four different kinds of nucleotides, so the simplest approach would be to have each nucleotide specify a different amino acid. That is, adenine would code for the amino acid glycine, cytosine for the amino acid lysine, and so on. This simple code may have been useful to the earliest cells, but it is limited to the construction of proteins consisting of only four different kinds of amino acids.

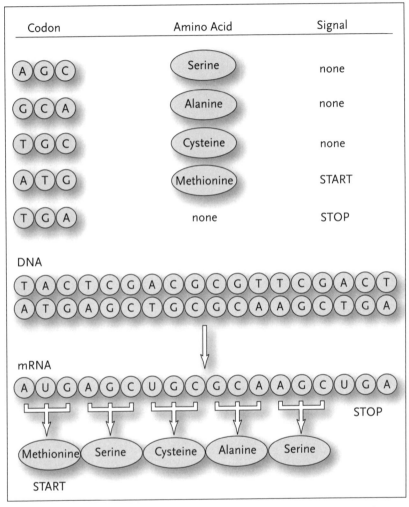

Transcription and the genetic code. Five codons are shown, four specifying amino acids (protein subunits) and two that serve as start and stop signals. The codons, including the start and stop signals, are linked together to form a gene on the bottom, or coding, DNA strand. The coding strand is copied into messenger RNA (mRNA), which is used to synthesize the protein. Nucleotides appear as round beads: Adenine (A), Thymine (T), Cytosine (C), and Guanine (G). Amino acids appear as labeled elliptical beads. Note that in mRNA, uracil (U) replaces the thymine (T) found in DNA.

Prokaryotes undoubtedly experimented with a variety of coding methods before adopting the current system, in which a combination of three out of the four possible DNA nucleotides, called a codon, specifies a single amino acid. With this scheme, it is possible to have a unique code for each of the 20 naturally occurring amino acids. For example, the codon AGC specifies the amino acid serine, whereas TGC specifies the amino acid cysteine. Codons are linked together to form a long continuous sequence that is called a gene. Not all the codons code for amino acids. The sequence TGA signals the end of the gene, and a special codon, ATG, signals the start site, in addition to specifying the amino acid methionine. Thus all proteins begin with this amino acid, although it is sometimes removed once construction of the protein is complete. An average protein may consist of 300 to 400 amino acids; since the codon consists of three nucleotides for each amino acid, a typical gene may be 900 to 1200 nucleotides long. The codon system, developed by the prokaryotes, is also used by the eukaryotes, and for this reason is referred to as the universal genetic code (see table on page 32).

Messenger RNA is the working copy of the gene, but it has the nucleotide uracil in place of thymine, which is found in DNA. Consequently, the DNA codon for methionine is ATG, but it is AUG on the mRNA. The ribosomal RNAs are programmed to recognize the codon as it appears on the mRNA. Once the protein is made, mRNA is broken down and the nucleotides recycled. Thus, mRNA has a very short life span, sometimes referred to as its half-life (the time it takes for half the population to disappear), which can range from a few seconds to a few hours. The short half-life of mRNA makes the cell very responsive to changing conditions in the environment and within the cell itself.

The complete genetic code used by all living things on this planet consists of 64 codons that specify 20 amino acids and the start and stop sites (see table on page 32). The large number of codons is due to redundancy in the code; that is, several codons may specify the same amino acid. Human carpenters, as mentioned previously, use a two-dimensional blueprint to build a three-dimensional house, but prokaryotes have gone us one better. They build three-dimensional objects (proteins), but they do it with a one-dimensional blueprint. Moreover, the invention of the codon, and the use of it to produce identical copies of the same protein over and over again, is nature's first and most important cloning experiment.

THE UNIVERSAL GENETIC CODE		
Codon	Amino Acid	Signal
GCA GCC GCG GCU	Alanine	–
UGC UGU	Cysteine	–
GAC GAU	Aspartic acid	–
GAA GAG	Glutamic acid	–
UUC UUU	Phenylalanine	–
GGA GGC GGG GGU	Glycine	–
CAC CAU	Histidine	–
AUA AUC AUU	Isoleucine	–
AAA AAG	Lysine	–
UUA UUG CUA CUC CUG CUU	Leucine	–
AUG	Methionine	Start
AAC AAU	Asparagine	–
CCA CCC CCG CCU	Proline	–
CAA CAG	Glutamine	–
AGA AGG CGA CGC CGG CGU	Arginine	–
AGC AGU UCA UCC UCG UCU	Serine	–
ACA ACC ACG ACU	Threonine	–
GUA GUC GUG GUU	Valine	–
UGG	Tryptophan	–
UAC UAU	Tyrosine	–
UAA UGA UAG	–	Stop

Codons are written using the standard abbreviation for each nucleotide on the messenger RNA: adenine (A), uracil (U), cytosine (C), and guanine (G). Note that in mRNA uracil replaces the thymine found in DNA.

The Good, the Bad, and the Ugly

The classification of bacteria is based on the cell's morphology, its motility, the way they grow on a culture plate, the kinds of sugars and other molecules that they are able to metabolize, and whether their metabolism is anaerobic or aerobic. In 1844, the Danish bacteriologist Hans Christian Gram introduced a simple staining procedure that provides a convenient way of distinguishing different types of bacteria that otherwise have the same physical appearance. The Gram stain exploits the chemical properties of the cell walls in different species of bacteria. Those bacteria that retain the stain, which is blue, are referred to as being Gram positive and those that do not are Gram negative. For example, *Myxobacteria, Staphylococcus,* and *Streptococcus* are Gram positive, whereas *Salmonella, Pseudomonas,* and *Cyanobacteria* are Gram negative. DNA sequence analysis of ribosomal RNA has also been used to assign cells to various taxonomic groups.

We generally think of bacteria in the context of a disease they are known to cause, and many of them do cause very serious disorders. But most bacteria fall into the "good" category and can be found living in the water and the soil, on our skin, and in our intestinal tracts. Indeed, there are even bacteria living among the clouds. Because trees and elephants are so big, we tend to think that they, along with other plants and animals, contribute the most to the biomass of the earth, but this is not the case. Bacteria not only outnumber us, they outweigh us by a wide margin.

Bacteria are always busy making a living, just as they have done for billions of years, and the thing that occupies most of their time is the extraction of energy from organic molecules. A by-product of the extraction process is the recycling of nutrients, an activity that is crucial to the maintenance of earth's ecosystem. Carbon and nitrogen compounds, essential for the synthesis of proteins and nucleic acids, would be lost from the system if not recycled by bacteria. In this regard, the cyanobacteria (sometimes called blue-green algae) are perhaps the most important. This is an extremely ancient group of filamentous bacteria (see table on page 34).

Fossilized remains of cyanobacteria date back nearly 3 billion years and are the oldest fossils known. The discovery of fossilized cyanobacteria was crucial to our understanding of the origin of life and the conditions prevalent on our primitive earth. Cyanobacteria are capable of photosynthesis and are believed to be the evolutionary forerunners of modern-day plant and algal chloroplasts. They are also important members of the phytoplankton in the oceans and freshwater lakes,

CHARACTERISTICS OF SOME COMMON BACTERIA

Good

Cyanobacteria	Gram-negative, aerobic, nonmotile short rods that occur singly, in long filaments and irregular colonies. Cells are capable of photosynthesis and live in freshwater and marine habitats. They recycle organic matter.
Myxobacteria	Gram-negative, aerobic, motile rods that occur singly but can aggregate to form fruiting bodies and spores. Cells live in the soil and have a complex life cycle. They recycle terrestrial organic matter and build soil.
Pseudomonas	Gram-negative, aerobic, motile (with several flagella) rods that occur singly or in pairs. Cells live in soil and water and are able to decompose virtually any organic molecule, including crude oil. Important as recyclers and soil builders.
Spirillum	Gram-negative, aerobic, motile (with a single flagella), long spiral-shaped rod that always occurs singly. Cells live in freshwater and marine habitats. They recycle organic matter.
Lactobacillus	Gram-positive, aerobic, non-spore-forming rods that occur singly. Important in the food industry for the production of cheese, yogurt, sour cream, and other dairy products.

accounting for more than 25 percent of the biomass produced in aquatic ecosystems.

Terrestrial counterparts to the cyanobacteria are the myxobacteria and the pseudomonads, both of which are important for their ability to recycle organic compounds and for making soil. The myxobacteria are especially interesting because of their complex social behavior that is unique among all of the prokaryotes. Myxobacteria live out most of their lives as vegetative cells that browse among the soil and leaf litter. If

Bad	
Salmonella	Gram-negative, aerobic, motile rods that occur singly. Two species, gallainarum and pullorum, cause food poisoning.
Streptococcus	Gram-positive, aerobic cocci (spheres) that occur singly or in short chains. Several species cause throat infections, tonsillitis, and food poisoning.
Staphylococcus	Gram-positive, aerobic cocci that occur singly or in grapelike clusters. S. aureus is a major cause of food poisoning. Symptoms are produced by a toxin.
Ugly	
Bacillus anthtracis	Gram-positive, aerobic, nonmotile rods that occur singly. These are spore-forming bacteria that germinate when inhaled by people or cattle. The cells attack the lungs and the disease is usually fatal.
Vibrio cholerae	Gram-negative, aerobic, curved rods that occur singly. Ecology similar to Pseudomonads. Causative agent of cholera, which is usually fatal if not treated promptly.
Neisseria gonorrhoeae	Gram-negative, aerobic, small cocci that occur in pairs. A major cause of sexually transmitted disease, affecting 3 million people a year. Infected pregnant women can pass it to their children, who develop serious eye infections if not treated promptly.

the food supply runs out, the cells aggregate at the top of the leaf litter, where they form a fruiting body that looks like a tiny cluster of grapes. Some of the cells form the stalk and storage capsules, called cysts, while the rest form the spores that become sealed inside the cysts (the grape-like structures). Being on top of the leaf litter exposes the fruiting body to the wind, which may carry some of the cysts to other areas where, hopefully, there is more food available. When the conditions are right, the cysts rupture, releasing the spores, which germinate into vegetative cells. This remarkable life cycle is an example of the kind of colonial behavior, adopted by primitive cells, that eventually led to the appearance of multicellular creatures.

Not all bacteria live in the soil, air, or water: Many live on the skin or inside the bodies of animals. Those that live inside an animal's body are restricted to the oral cavity, the throat, and the digestive tract. For the most part, these bacteria are harmless, sometimes even beneficial. But there are a few that can make people and animals very sick, and in some

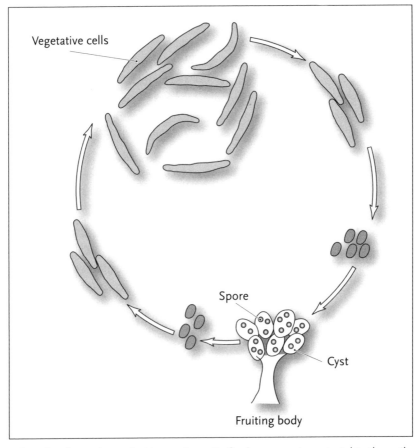

Life cycle of myxobacteria. Vegetative cells feed on organic material in the soil. When food runs low, the cells are stimulated to form a fruiting body consisting of many cysts, which are full of spores. When conditions are favorable, the cysts break open and the spores germinate into vegetative cells.

cases the disease can be fatal. Some of the "bad" bacteria that we have to contend with are species from the *Salmonella, Streptococcus,* and *Staphylococcus* genera, which cause food poisoning and, in the case of *Streptococcus,* serious throat infections. Although these bacteria can make people very sick, the diseases they produce are mild compared with those produced by the "ugly" bacteria.

The most notorious among this latter group is *Bacillus anthracis,* a spore-forming bacterium responsible for anthrax, a disease affecting cattle and humans. When an animal inhales *B. anthracis* spores, it is like offering the bacteria a large plate of food. The spores germinate very quickly into vegetative cells and begin consuming the victim's lung tissue. Death usually follows within a few days. Antibiotics are available for this disease but are usually ineffective unless given to the patient on the day the spores are inhaled.

Bacillus anthracis has recently been used by bioterrorists, who have exploited the deadliness of the disease and the hardiness of the anthrax spores, which can remain viable for years. The spores, which to the naked eye look like a fine powder, were used in 2001 to contaminate letters before they were sent to various destinations in the United States. Several people died of an anthrax infection after being exposed to some of those letters.

·3·

EUKARYOTES

Dawn of a New Era

The only thing in nature more complicated than a eukaryote is a bunch of eukaryotes working together; the heart is one example, the human brain is another. The complexity of these cells came about as a result of necessity and the struggle for survival. Life began in coastal waters that were filled with nutrients, produced by the heat and storms of pre-biotic earth. As the first cells consumed those nutrients, selection pressures led to the appearance of phototrophic prokaryotes, known as autotrophs, that could obtain their energy through photosynthesis. But many prokaryotes, known as heterotrophs, lacked this ability and in order to survive began hunting other prokaryotes for food. Scientists believe the eukaryotes evolved from this latter group of hunting heterotrophs. The new adaptations not only helped the eukaryotes hunt down their prey but also made it possible for those cells to communicate with one another and, eventually, to form colonies and multicellular creatures.

The emergence of the eukaryotes was an important event, not only because a new lifeform had emerged, but also for the survival of the entire ecosystem. Eukaryotes went on to produce enormous populations of photosynthetic organisms both in the water and on the land. Decomposing land plants and animal excretions produced soil, which in turn provides a habitat for billions of prokaryotes and other creatures. These habitats could not have been produced by prokaryotes alone. Thus it is possible that without the eukaryotes, life may have died out on this planet sometime after the first cells consumed the prebiotic nutri-

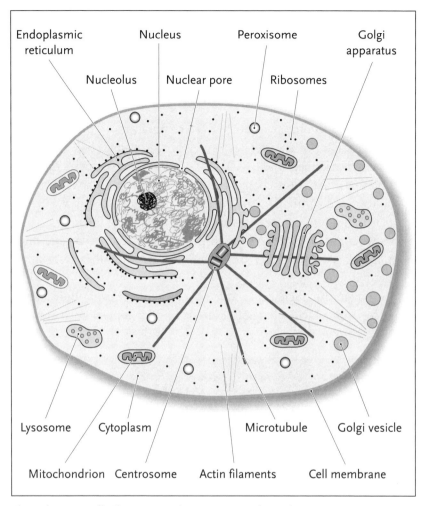

The eukaryote cell. The structural components shown here are present in organisms as diverse as protozoans, plants, and animals. The nucleus contains the DNA genome and an assembly plant for ribosomal subunits (the nucleolus). The endoplasmic reticulum (ER) and the Golgi work together to modify proteins, most of which are destined for the cell membrane. These proteins are sent to the membrane in Golgi vesicles. Mitochondria provide the cell with energy in the form of ATP. Ribosomes, some of which are attached to the ER, synthesize proteins. Lysosomes and peroxisomes recycle cellular material and molecules. The microtubules and centrosome form the spindle apparatus for moving chromosomes to the daughter cells during cell division. Actin filaments, and a weblike structure consisting of intermediate filaments (not shown), form the cytoskeleton.

ents. Eukaryotes took the evolution of life to a new level, and the adaptations that made this possible, and that distinguish them from the prokaryotes, are the subject of this chapter.

Overview of Eukaryote Structure and Function

Eukaryotes (meaning "true nucleus") are much more complex than prokaryotes. The prokaryotes keep everything in a single bag. Genes are replicated, transcribed, and translated all in one compartment, the cell's protoplasm. Eukaryotes changed all this by setting up special membrane-bounded compartments, or organelles, for each job. While the cytoplasm of a prokaryote is plain and homogeneous, the interior of a eukaryote is a maze of organelles, which includes the nucleus, nucleolus, endoplasmic reticulum (ER), Golgi complex, mitochondria, lysosomes, and peroxisomes.

The eukaryote nucleus, bounded by a double phospholipid membrane, contains a DNA (deoxyribonucleic acid) genome on two or more

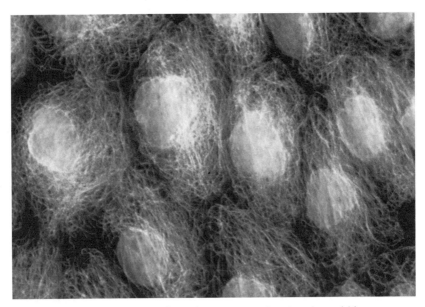

Micrograph of epithelial cells from the pancreas showing the weblike structure of the cytoskeleton. Magnification: 2520x. *(Courtesy of Jennifer Waters Shuler/ Photo Researchers, Inc.)*

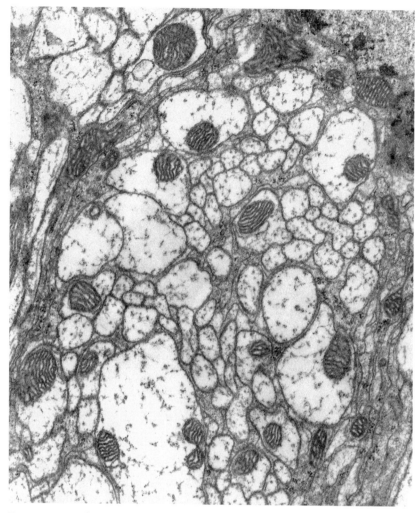

Transmission electron micrograph (TEM) of a section of housefly brain showing the large number of mitochondria that is typical of extremely active tissue. Magnification: 19,250x. *(Courtesy of Dr. Joseph Panno)*

linear chromosomes, each of which may contain thousands of genes. The nucleus also contains an assembly plant for ribosomal subunits, called the nucleolus. The ER and the Golgi complex work together to glycosylate proteins and lipids (attach sugar molecules to the proteins and lipids producing glycoproteins and glycolipids), most of which are

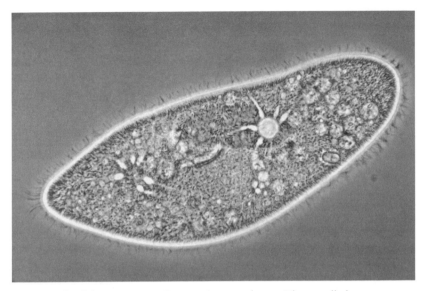

Micrograph of the protozoan *Paramecium candatum*. These cells have a characteristic shape of a slipper, and their outer surface is covered in cilia. The cell interior is filled with circular food vacuoles. The bright star-shaped structures are contractile vacuoles, and the macronucleus can be seen lying below the one to the right. Magnification: 160x. *(Courtesy of M.I. Walker/Photo Researchers, Inc.)*

destined for the cell membrane to form a molecular "forest" known as the glycocalyx. The glycoproteins and glycolipids travel from the ER to the Golgi, and from the Golgi to the cell surface, in membrane-bounded vesicles (bubbles) that form by budding off the organelle by exocytosis. Thus the cytoplasm contains many transport vesicles that originate from the ER and Golgi. The Golgi vesicles bud off the outer chamber, or the one farthest from the ER. Mitochondria, once free-living prokaryotes, and the only other organelle with a double membrane, provide the cell with energy in the form of adenosine triphosphate (ATP). The production of ATP is carried out by an assembly of metal-containing proteins, called the electron transport chain, located in the mitochondrion inner membrane. Ribosomes, some of which are attached to the ER, synthesize proteins. Lysosomes and peroxisomes recycle cellular material and molecules. The microtubules and centrosome form the spindle apparatus for moving chromosomes to the daughter cells during cell division.

Actin filaments, and a weblike structure consisting of intermediate filaments, form the cytoskeleton.

The functional organization of a eukaryote is similar to a carpentry shop. Imagine such a place, where carpenters use a copy of a master blueprint, stored in the shop's office, to build wooden chairs; this shop builds many different kinds of chairs, and it keeps a blueprint for each one. All the machines and tools the carpenters use to build the chairs are located on the shop floor. Every morning, someone in the office takes a blueprint out of the filing cabinet, makes a photocopy of it, and then takes it out to the shop floor and gives it to one of the carpenters. This blueprint may represent a standing order, or the shop may have received an order that morning to produce a special chair. After the chairs are made, some of the carpenters take them into a finishing room, where the frames are painted, after which they go to a shipping room, where they are packaged and sent out to the shop's customers. The energy to power the tools, and to heat and illuminate the shop, comes from electricity, produced at a hydroelectric dam. The shop communicates with its customers, and with other shops, by using the telephone or by sending a letter or an e-mail.

In a eukaryote cell, the shop floor is the cytoplasm and the shop office is the nucleus. The blueprints for everything that the cell makes are kept in the nucleus, but instead of being pictures on a piece of paper, they are made out of DNA. The cell makes proteins of various kinds, and it keeps a blueprint for each one. The blueprints are genes that are arranged, end-to-end, on a very long molecule of DNA. That molecule is the chromosome, and eukaryotes always have more than one.

A eukaryote makes copies of some of its genes every day. Each copy is called a messenger RNA (mRNA), and after being delivered to the cytoplasm, it is used to guide the production of a protein. The cell's carpenters are enzymes that use translation machinery in the cytoplasm to build the proteins. Some of the proteins remain in the cytoplasm to help run the cell, but most are sent to the ER, analogous to the finishing room, where they are glycosylated (painted with sugar), and then to the Golgi complex, where they mature before being packaged for export. These structures, the ER and the Golgi complex, have no counterparts among the prokaryotes. The sugar-coated (glycosylated) proteins from the Golgi are sent to the cell surface, where they form the glycocalyx. As described in chapter 2, the trunks of the trees in this forest are made from protein and the leaves are made from sugar molecules (the "glyco" part). The glycocalyx is part of the cell's communication hardware, allowing it to send and receive messages. Cell-surface glycoproteins also form the transporters and ion channels that serve as gateways into the cell. Prokaryotes have a glycocalyx, but its form and function are very simple by comparison. Eukaryotes have refined this hardware to such an extent that a neuron in the human brain can send a signal to the big toe in a fraction of a second. Eukaryotes, like carpentry shops, consume a great deal of energy every day. Carpentry shops get their energy from a hydroelectric dam, whereas eukaryotes get their power from the mitochondria. A hydroelectric dam supplies power in the form of electrons, but mitochondria supply it in the form ATP.

Although organized like a carpentry shop, the internal structure of a eukaryote is more like that of a coral reef. The cell's "reef" consists of the ER and the Golgi complex; the ER being the larger of the two, fanning out from the nucleus like the rings of Saturn. A real coral reef is a very busy place, with a multitude of colorful fish going about their daily business. Traffic in and around the Golgi complex and the ER is equally hectic, with thousands of multicolored proteins, RNAs, and smaller molecules speeding around as they take care of a thousand chores each day. Traffic between the Golgi complex and the cell membrane alone consists of a constant stream of millions of transport bubbles.

The behavior of eukaryote enzymes, particularly in the nucleus, is akin to that of shepherds tending their flock. Chromosomes, for example, are the most passive macromolecules in the cell, and they are tended by a special group of enzymes that act very much like shepherds. The enzymes move the chromosomes around in preparation for cell division, they regulate the duplication (replication) of each chromosome and the copying of each gene (transcription), and they are constantly inspecting the chromosomes for damage, repairing them when necessary. Why do these molecular shepherds spend so much time and energy caring for the chromosomes? The relationship between DNA and enzymes is an example of the most ancient and most successful cloning experiment. Enzymes have short lives, but a new and exact copy can always be produced as long as the genes are cared for and kept in good shape.

The Nucleus

The nucleus houses the chromosomes and all the enzymes necessary to replicate, transcribe, and repair the genes. The complexity of a eukaryote, compared with a prokaryote, suggests a larger genome, and this has been confirmed with the completion of the human genome project and the sequencing of several prokaryote genomes. Bacteria usually have 2,000 to 4,000 genes, compared with 30,000 in the human genome. This one difference is at the heart of all the other differences between the prokaryotes and the eukaryotes.

Prokaryotes pack all their genes onto a single, ring-shaped chromosome, but a structure such as this could not be used to store 30,000 genes. Eukaryotes solved this problem by splitting their genome into several linear chromosomes. Human cells, for example, have 46 chromosomes, 23 originating from the mother and 23 from the father. Each chromosome is a single, extremely long DNA molecule. This type of chromosome solves the problem of storing a large number of genes, but it becomes a problem when the cell tries to divide. Imagine unwinding and untangling 46 pieces of thread, each of which is several miles long, so they can be laid out, side-by-side, in nice, even rows. The chromosomes have to be aligned in this way for the successful completion of the cell cycle (chapter 4).

Moving long genetic threads around is a major problem but one that eukaryotes solved by coating their chromosomes with special proteins, called histones, that can be manipulated with phosphokinases (enzymes that phosphorylate or add phosphate groups to proteins). Consequently, the chromosome of a eukaryote is not naked DNA, as is that of a prokaryote. There are several kinds of histones, most of which form a spherical structure called a nucleosome that makes the relaxed chromosome look like a string of beads. The complex of DNA and histones is called chromatin. Phosphorylating the nucleosomes is like releasing a stretched rubber band: The chromosome contracts to form a compact structure that is 10,000 times shorter than the bare piece of DNA. Just as a suitcase makes it possible for us to take our clothes on a trip, histones and the chromatin structure they produce make it possible for the cell to package its genes in preparation for cell division.

Chromatin compaction, or condensation, is also used during interphase (the period between cell divisions) to help manage the

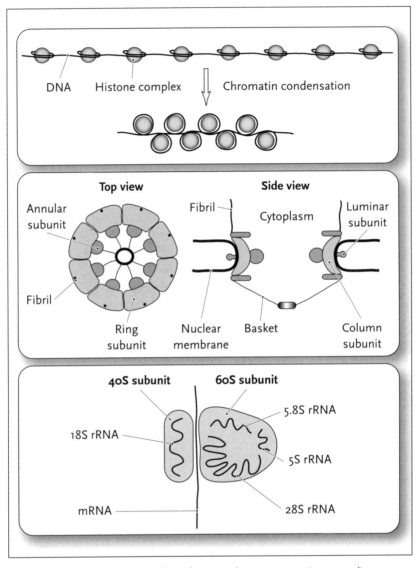

Components of a eukaryote cell. Eukaryote chromosomes (top panel) are a complex of DNA and histones, called chromatin, that exists in extended and condensed states. The nuclear pore (middle panel) is an octagonal structure built from many protein subunits that provide a channel through the nuclear membrane. The ribosome (bottom panel) consists of two protein subunits (40S, 60S) that are associated with different ribosomal RNAs (rRNA). Translation is initiated when the two subunits bind to messenger RNA (mRNA).

chromosomes and as one mechanism for controlling gene expression. The packing ratio of interphase chromatin is about 1:1,000 overall, but there are regions where it can be much lower (the density increases as the ratio decreases). This variation in the density of the chromatin accounts for the blotchy appearance of most interphase nuclei. Areas of the nucleus that are very dark present highly compacted chromatin, whereas the lighter regions contain chromatin in a more relaxed state. At the molecular level, chromatin condensation is an extremely dynamic process that is used to close down single genes or whole neighborhoods consisting of hundreds of genes. The mechanism by which this occurs is fairly straightforward: highly condensed chromatin blocks the transcription machinery, so it cannot get access to the gene. Details of this mechanism, and others that control gene expression, will be covered in chapter 5.

Keeping the genes in one compartment and the protein manufacturing machinery in another compartment requires a constant flow of traffic across the nuclear envelope. This traffic is not just the mRNA moving out to the cytoplasm; it also includes the millions of proteins that are synthesized in the cytoplasm but stationed inside the nucleus. Histones, for example, must be imported at a rate of 1 million every three minutes. DNA replication and repair enzymes, and the protein components of the ribosome, which are assembled in the nucleolus, are also part of the traffic.

Eukaryotes evolved an adjustable nuclear pore with an exquisite octagonal geometry to cope with all the traffic moving in and out of the nucleus (see the figure on page 46). The pore is constructed from four subunits, each of which is composed of more than one kind of protein, and basketlike assembly on the nuclear side. All together, nearly 50 different kinds of protein are used to construct this pore, and a typical cell has 3,000 to 4,000 of them, evenly spaced over the surface of the nuclear envelope. At certain magnifications, the pores make the nuclear envelope look like the crater-marked surface of the moon (although, unlike moon craters, nuclear "craters" are all the same size).

The nuclear pore blocks the passage by simple diffusion of any molecule larger than nine nanometers (nm, 10^{-9} meters) in diameter. Nuclear proteins that are larger than this gain access by a specific interaction with the cytosolic fibrils that causes the pore to open, somewhat like the iris diaphragm of a camera, just enough to let the molecule in. Scientists know the interaction between the protein and the fibril involves a nuclear localization sequence (NLS) on the protein itself, and without it, the pore will not allow the protein to pass. The NLS is like a password or a passport written in the language of an amino acid sequence, usually located at the very end of the protein. A common password for a nuclear protein is Lysine-lysine-lysine-arginine-lysine. If a nuclear protein presented itself to a nuclear pore with a mutated password, such as Lysine-threonine-lysine-arginine-lysine, it would not get in. Scientists have been able to trick the nuclear pore by adding the correct password to a protein that does not normally belong in the nucleus. Such experiments have made it clear that the pore checks the password only and does not care about the identity of the protein. The mechanism by which the pore is able to recognize the correct password and vary the diameter of its channel accordingly is still a mystery.

Protein Synthesis

Eukaryotes synthesize their proteins using ribosomes and the genetic code, just as prokaryotes do. But (as explained in chapter 2) ribosomes are constructed from a mixture of protein and RNA, and this fact created a problem for the eukaryotes. The RNA is made in the nucleus, but the protein is made in the cytoplasm: Where should the ribosome be made? The RNA could be synthesized and shipped out to the cytoplasm, where the ribosome could be assembled, or the protein components could be shipped into the nucleus for final assembly. But given that mRNA is also synthesized there, assembly of the ribosome in the nucleus could lead to a real disaster. If the ribosomes encountered the mRNA, the cell would end up synthesizing proteins in both the nucleus and the cytoplasm, which is exactly what the two compartments were designed to prevent. What a quandary! One solution would be to remake the ribosome so it is all protein or all RNA. However, this would be a formidable task because the ribosome is a very complex structure that took many millions of years to evolve.

To appreciate the complexity of the ribosome, let us examine its components. The eukaryote ribosome consists of two major complexes, called the 40S and 60S subunits (the *S* refers to their rate of sedimentation

in a centrifuge; the larger the S value, the larger the rRNA). The 40S subunit consists of 33 proteins and a single 18S (having 1,900 nucleotides)
ribosomal RNA molecule (rRNA). The 60S subunit has 50 proteins and
three different rRNA molecules that range in size from 120 nucleotides
(5S) to 4,700 nucleotides (28S). A functional ribosome is produced
when the 40S and 60S subunits bind to an mRNA. After translating the
mRNA to produce a protein molecule, the ribosomal subunits dissociate from the mRNA (see figure on page 46).

Trying to re-create such a complex structure is out of the question.
Instead, the eukaryotes settled on a compromise strategy to keep the
ribosome as it is (although they did add a few extra proteins and one
extra RNA molecule), and to assemble the subunits in the nucleus but
not join them together there. Subunit assembly occurs in the nucleolus,
where the rRNAs are synthesized and where ribosomal proteins collect
after entering the nucleus from the cytoplasm. Once assembled, the
inactive subunits can be safely transported to a pore. Biologists believe
the final activation of each subunit occurs as they pass through separate
nuclear pores. Once they are in the cytoplasm, they are free to associate
with mRNA to initiate translation.

Designing a Molecular Forest

The eukaryote glycocalyx is more complex than the one produced by
prokaryotes. Prokaryotes use the glycocalyx to collect and import food
molecules, whereas the eukaryotes use it both for food collection and
for cell-to-cell communication. Consequently, the eukaryote glycocalyx
has a much more diverse collection of glycoproteins embedded in the
membrane, and there is a higher proportion of glycolipids, particularly
in nerve cells. The production of glycoproteins in prokaryotes occurs in
the cytoplasm, but in eukaryotes they are produced in the ER and the
Golgi complex.

Proteins destined for the cell membrane carry a marker sequence,
much in the way nuclear proteins carry an NLS. When the ribosome
detects the marker sequence, it moves to the surface of the ER where it
threads the protein through a pore as it is being synthesized. Ribosomes,
located on the surface of the ER, can be clearly seen in electron micro-
graphs; those areas are referred to as the rough ER. Once the protein is

inside the ER, it is glycosylated by several different enzymes that add the sugar molecules sequentially. This is analogous to a team of painters working on the same canvas. One painter might lay in the sky and

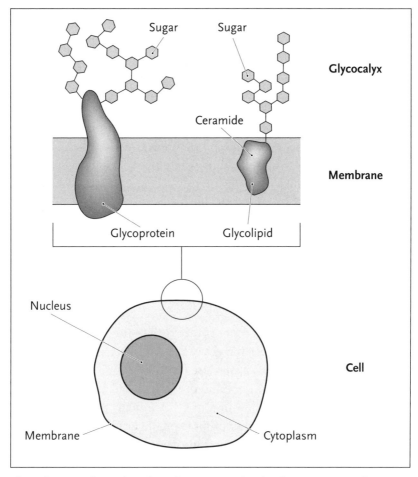

The eukaryote glycocalyx. The eukaryote's molecular forest consists of glycoproteins and glycolipids. Two examples are shown at the top, a glycoprotein on the left and a glycolipid on the right. The glycoprotein trees have "trunks" made of protein and "leaves" made of sugar molecules. Glycolipids also have "leaves" made of sugar molecules, but the "trunks" are a fatty compound called ceramide that is completely submerged within the plane of the membrane. The glycocalyx has many jobs, including cell-to-cell communication, and the transport and detection of food molecules. It also provides recognition markers so the immune system can detect foreign cells.

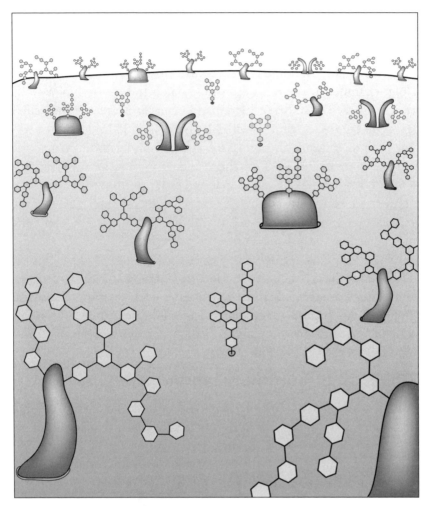

A panoramic view of the glycocalyx. The glycoproteins in the cell's forest come in many different shapes and sizes, and they dominate the surface of most cells. The glycolipids all have the same ceramide trunks, but the molecular foliage varies considerably. All but four of the structures in this image are glycoproteins, but in nerve cells they are much more common.

ground, after which another paints the clouds and rocks. The glycosylating enzymes seem to follow a set of rules, because the same kinds of glycoproteins are produced over and over again, but the nature of those rules is still unclear. When the enzymes in the ER are finished, the glycoprotein is loaded into a transport vesicle (bubble) and sent to the Golgi complex.

The Golgi complex has its own group of enzymes that specialize in refining the process begun in the ER. They begin by adding more sugar molecules, and as the glycoprotein (now looking very much like a molecular tree) is modified by successive enzymes, it moves from one Golgi chamber to the next, each time being transported by a Golgi vesicle. In each chamber, enzymes add, trim, or prune the molecular leaves on the trees. Again, as with ER glycosylation, the decision-making process guiding these tasks is poorly understood. When the enzymes are satisfied with the shape and appearance of the glycoprotein, it is loaded into a Golgi vesicle and sent out from the *trans* Golgi network (the outermost chamber) to the cell membrane. Fusion of the vesicle membrane with the cell membrane automatically plants the molecular tree.

Not all the glycoproteins that pass through the ER or Golgi are destined for the cell membrane. Many are intended for the lysosomes, and some are secreted. Indeed, Golgi vesicles carrying lysosomal glycoproteins become that organelle, as will be described later in this chapter.

The Birth of Communication

Eukaryotes expend a tremendous amount of time and energy building and maintaining the glycocalyx, a molecular forest that would, if we were small enough to walk through it, rival the beauty of any forest on the surface of the Earth. Despite this, eukaryotes build the glycocalyx not because they want to look good but because they need to communicate with their environment, and especially with other cells. The glycoproteins in the cell's forest come in many different shapes and sizes, but functionally they all fall within one of three groups: transporters, ion channels, and receptors.

Transporters are designed to carry specific molecules (usually food of some kind) across the cell membrane. Each type of molecule, such as glucose, lactose, and amino acids, has its own transporter. The intestinal tract, which absorbs the nutrients from the food we eat, has an enormous population of each kind of transporter. Virtually all the nutrients are taken into intestinal cells by transporters and then released into the blood by transporters working in reverse, that is, moving molecules from inside the cell to the outside (into the circulatory system). Other tissues of the body also have transporters. Most animal cells use glucose as their primary source of energy; this is particularly true of the brain. Consequently, all the tissues in an animal's body have a great number

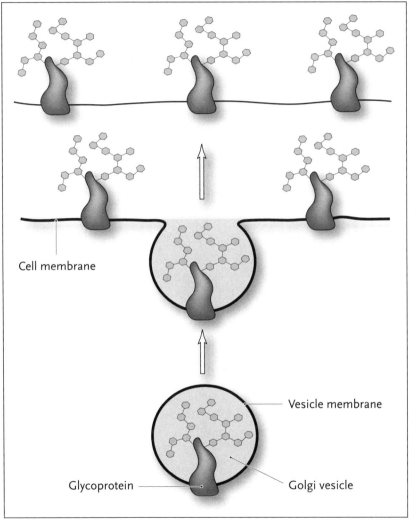

Cell membrane

Vesicle membrane

Glycoprotein

Golgi vesicle

Planting a molecular forest. Vesicles from the Golgi complex carry glycoproteins to the cell surface. Fusion of the vesicle membrane with the cell membrane automatically plants the molecular tree.

of glucose transporters (other sugars, brought in by the intestinal cells, are converted to glucose before being released into general circulation, so other kinds of sugar transporters are not needed outside the intestinal tract).

The second group of glycoproteins, the ion channels, represent a very powerful messaging system that uses the flow of ions into the cell as a means of communication; much in the way we use the flow of electrons down a phone line to speak with someone at a great distance. Ion channels are gated, that is, they can be opened and closed. Ligand-gated ion channels open when a signaling molecule binds to the channel. Voltage-gated channels open when they sense, or are jolted by, an electric field across the membrane.

Receptors, the third group of cell-surface glycoproteins, are the most diverse group of cell-surface glycoproteins and, along with ion channels, are at the heart of the cell's ability to communicate with other cells. Each receptor is designed to respond to a specific signaling molecule. When a signaling molecule binds to its receptor, it sets off a chain of biochemical events in the recipient, or target cell. The signal may cause the cell to increase or decrease the output of a product that is required by other cells in the body, or it may order the cell to grow, to stop growing, or even to commit suicide.

The most common type of receptor that cells use for communication is the G-protein linked receptor. A G-protein is an enzyme that gets its power from an energy reservoir called guanosine triphosphate (GTP), a close relative of the cell's main energy reservoir, adenosine triphosphate (ATP). Binding of a signaling molecule to one of these receptors leads to the activation of the G-protein, which in turn activates a transduction, or signal conversion, enzyme. This enzyme, in turn, produces or activates secondary messengers that cause the cell to carry out the appropriate response. This chain of events, from the moment the signaling molecule binds to its receptor, is called a signal transduction pathway. Alternatively, some signaling pathways use an enzyme-linked receptor, effectively cutting out the G-protein middleman. In a pathway such as this, the receptor itself is also a transduction enzyme, which is activated by the binding of a signaling molecule. The activated receptor phosphorylates, and thereby activates, secondary

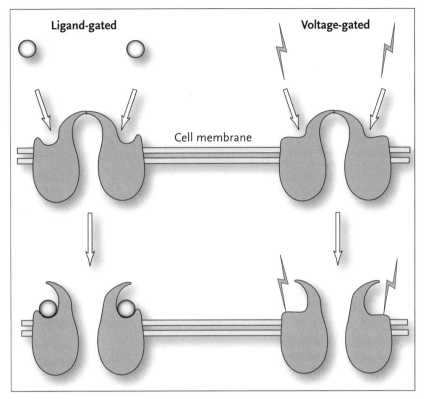

Ion channels. Ligand-gated channels open when bound to a signaling molecule, and voltage-gated channels open when they receive an electric jolt. Ion channels are glycoproteins that are an important part of the glycocalyx.

messengers that lead to a change in the activity or behavior of the target cell.

In a multicellular organism, such as a mouse or a human, communication is taken care of by the nervous system, using a combination of ligand-gated and voltage-gated ion channels, or by the endocrine system, which releases hormones as signals to other cells. These two systems coordinate virtually everything that goes on in an animal's body. The exquisite regulation of ion channels in neurons gives us our intellect, vision, hearing, and all other sensory perceptions. The endocrine system regulates our growth, sexual maturation, general energy levels, and even our mood from one day to the next (the function of neurons, and cell communication in general, will be described in greater detail in chapter 7). The regulation and coordination of ion channels for the purpose of cell-to-cell communication has no counterpart among the prokaryotes.

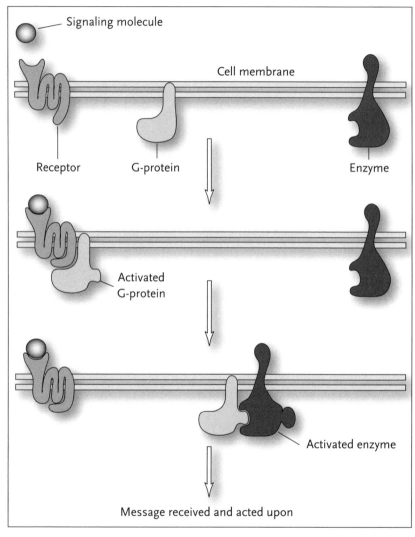

G-protein-linked receptor. The signaling molecule binds to the receptor, leading to the activation of the G-protein, which in turn activates an enzyme. The enzyme activates secondary messengers, which effect some change in the cell.

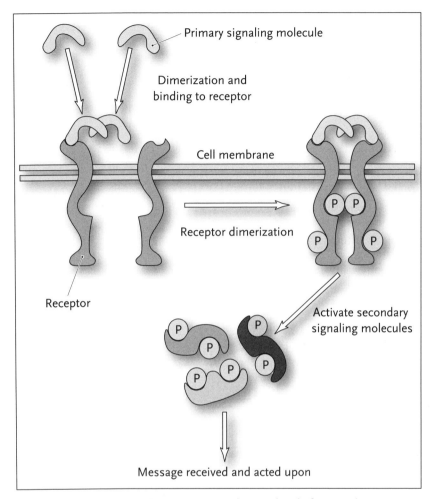

Primary signaling molecule

Dimerization and
binding to receptor

Cell membrane

Receptor dimerization

Receptor

Activate secondary
signaling molecules

Message received and acted upon

Enzyme-linked receptor. The primary signaling molecule forms a dimer (two identical molecules bound together) and binds to the receptor, stimulating dimerization of the receptor. This stimulates phosphokinase activity of the receptor, which phosphorylates itself and several secondary signaling molecules. The activated signaling molecules effect some change in the cell.

Symbiosis and the Quest for Power

As described in chapter 2, prokaryotes developed two aerobic systems for extracting energy from food molecules: the Krebs cycle, which stores most of the energy as electrons, and the electron transport chain, which uses the energy to make ATP. In eukaryotes, both processes occur in an organelle called the mitochondrion. Consequently, these organelles are responsible for providing the cell with the ATP it needs to power all its biochemical reactions (although a small amount of ATP is provided by glycolysis, which is carried out in the cell's cytoplasm).

For many years, cell biologists believed the mitochondria originated with the eukaryotes, but in 1910, the Russian biologist Konstantin Mereschovsky suggested that these organelles were once free-living prokaryotes. The earliest evidence in support of this notion, presented by the American biologist Lynn Margulis in 1970, focused on the fact that mitochondria have their own genome and are morphologically similar to bacteria. Since then, Margulis and others have described several interesting similarities between mitochondria and prokaryotes:

- ❏ Mitochondria divide by simple binary fission, as do bacteria.
- ❏ Synthesis of ATP occurs through the same pathway used by bacteria.
- ❏ Mitochondria and bacteria both have a single, circular DNA chromosome.
- ❏ The mitochondrial genome is very similar in structure and organization to that of many bacteria.

Today most scientists accept the symbiogenesis theory, which states that the evolution of eukaryotes was associated with the acquisition of symbionts, particularly mitochondria (in animals) and chloroplasts (in plants), about 2 billion years ago. Consequently, mitochondria have been handed down from one generation to the next ever since that time. In addition, for all the animals in the world, inheritance of mitochondria is through the maternal line. We get our mitochondria from our mothers. This fact has been applied by scientists at the University of California, Berkeley, who traced the origins of the human species to a single "mitochondrial Eve" who apparently lived in Africa 100,000 to 200,000 years ago.

Recycling and Defense

The lysosome is a cell organelle that is responsible for recycling worn-out cell parts, such as mitochondria, membranes, and various molecules. Lysosomes are vesicles that are filled with powerful enzymes that can break down virtually any structure or component of the cell. Lysosomal enzymes are glycoproteins that are sent through the ER and Golgi complex, but the Golgi vesicles containing these enzymes stay in the cytoplasm (rather than fusing with the cell membrane), where they mature into functional lysosomes.

Lysosomes are also very important for maintaining the cell membrane and other membrane-bounded structures. Traffic through the ER and the Golgi complex results in the fusion of ER vesicles with the Golgi and the fusion of Golgi vesicles with the cell membrane. If steps were not taken to recycle parts of both membrane systems they would grow very large, very quickly. In the case of the cell membrane, regular rounds of endocytosis serve to keep the membrane at a constant size. The endocytotic vesicle is fused with a lysosome where the parts are broken down, with some being returned to the Golgi and ER.

Cellular defense among animals is usually left to the immune system. But each cell does have built-in defense capabilities, left over from the time when cells were free living. This defense mechanism involves a coordination between the lysosomes and endocytosis. One form of endocytosis, called phagocytosis, makes it possible for the cell to engulf an invading bacterium. The phagocytic vesicle containing the bacterium fuses with a lysosome and breaks down the microbe to individual molecules, which are released into the cytoplasm or expelled from the cell. All eukaryotes have this defensive capability, but it is used most effectively by macrophages, an important cellular member of an animal's immune system.

The emergence of the eukaryotes came with the appearance of a super cell, about 2 billion years ago, that was 10 times larger than an average prokaryote. In addition, eukaryotes have 10 times the number of genes found in a typical prokaryote, and a complex and highly organized set of organelles that maximize the efficiency of basic manufacturing processes. The main priority of a eukaryote is the construction of a highly complex glycocalyx. The eukaryote glycocalyx greatly improves the efficiency of food gathering, particularly for single-cell eukaryotes that have a predator lifestyle. The improved glycocalyx also made it possible for eukaryotes to communicate with each other, and this capability paved the way for cell colonies and, eventually, true multicellular organisms.

·4·

THE CELL CYCLE

Cells inherited the power of reproduction from the prebiotic bubbles that split in half at regular intervals, under the influence of their turbulent environment. This pattern of turbulent fragmentation followed by a brief period of calm is now stuck in the molecular psyche, or behavior pattern, of every cell. Even today, after 3 billion years, many bacteria still divide every 20 minutes. Though eukaryotes take longer to divide, their regularity is just as profound.

The regular alternation between division and calm has come to be known as the cell cycle. In studying this cycle, scientists have recognized different states of calm and different ways in which a cell can divide. The calm state of the cell cycle, referred to as interphase, is divided into three subphases called Gap 1 (G_1), S phase (a period of DNA synthesis), and Gap 2 (G_2). The conclusion of interphase, and with it the termination of G_2, occurs with the division of the cell and a return to G_1. Cells may leave the cycle by entering a special phase called G_0. Some cells, such as post-mitotic neurons in an animal's brain, remain in G_0 for the life of the organism.

Although interphase is a period of relative calm, the cell grows continuously during this period, working hard to prepare for the next round of division. Two notable events are the duplication of the spindle (the centrosome and associated microtubules), a structure that is crucial for the movement of the chromosomes during cell division, and the appearance of an enzyme called maturation-promoting factor (MPF) at the end of G_2. MPF is the enzyme that phosphorylates the histones in order to compact the chromosomes in preparation for cell division. MPF is also responsible for the breakdown of the nuclear membrane. When cell division is complete, MPF disappears, allowing the chromosomes to decondense and the nuclear envelope to re-form.

Many of the events that occur during interphase are poorly understood, but we do know the intention of all the labor is to ensure the production of two identical daughter cells. When the prebiotic bubbles divided, the two new bubbles were not necessarily identical to each other, as there were no mechanisms in place to ensure an equal distribution of the parent bubble's contents. The dissimilarity of the daughter bubbles was an advantage at that stage of development, but true cells had too much to lose to permit haphazard divisions. Thus, the appearance of true cells required mechanisms that guaranteed identical daughter cells.

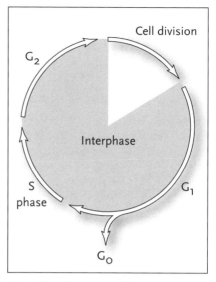

The cell cycle. Most cells spend their time cycling between a state of calm (interphase) and cell division. Interphase is further divided into three subphases: Gap 1 (G_1), S phase (DNA synthesis), and Gap 2 (G_2). Cells may exit the cycle by entering a special phase called G_0.

Natural selection is the driving force behind the appearance of novel cellular mechanisms. If a cell happened on to a useful biochemical reaction, there would have been a strong selection pressure to preserve that innovation by providing a way for that cell to hand it down to succeeding generations. The acquisition of new traits and abilities is always linked to the appearance of enzymes with new talents. The earliest cells had already begun storing genetic information for their enzymes, first as an RNA genome and later as DNA. The problem they faced initially was the need to duplicate their genome accurately and to coordinate that process with cell division in order to ensure the production of identical daughter cells.

DNA Replication

To understand how a cell duplicates its genome during S phase, it is necessary to understand something about the structure of a nucleotide and the way in which several nucleotides are linked together to form a single-stranded DNA molecule. Nucleotides, shown in the figure below, are linked together to form single-stranded

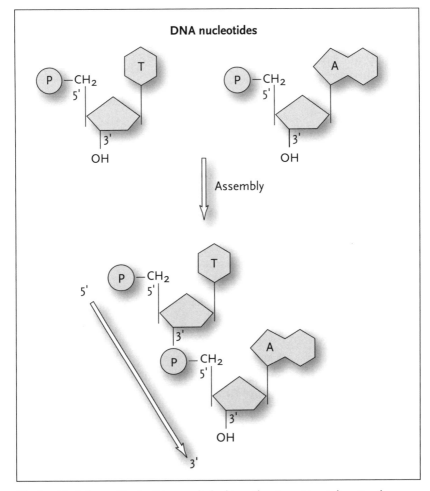

Nucleotide linkage. Nucleotides are linked together in a 5' to 3' direction by linking the phosphate of the adenine (A) nucleotide to the 3' carbon of the thymine (T) nucleotide. The OH group on the T nucleotide is lost in the process.

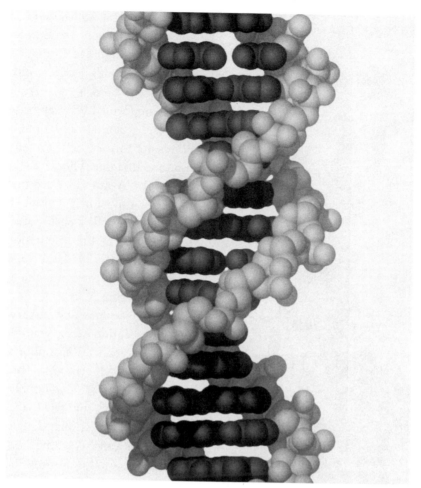

Computer model of DNA. The two strands coil around each other to form a helix that, when looking down on it from above, coils to the right. The spherical structures in this image represent the various atoms in the sugars and bases (dark gray), and phosphates (light gray). *(Courtesy of Kenneth Eward/BioGrafx/Photo Researchers, Inc.)*

DNA by the attachment of the phosphate group of one nucleotide to the 3' carbon of a second nucleotide. Since the phosphate of the first nucleotide is attached to its 5' carbon, the DNA chain is said to grow in the 5' to 3' direction. The internal OH group is lost when the two nucleotides are joined together.

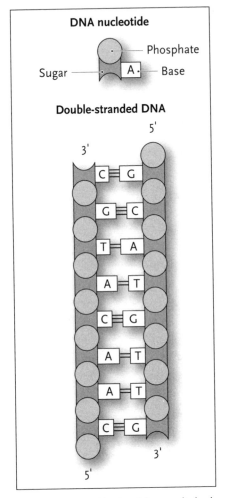

DNA nucleotide

Phosphate

Sugar — A — Base

Double-stranded DNA

DNA structure. Nucleotides are linked together to form a double-stranded molecule. The bases are held together with double or triple bonds, and the two strands are antiparallel.

Double-stranded DNA forms when two chains of nucleotides interact through the formation of chemical bonds between complementary base pairs. Triple bonds are formed between cytosine and guanine, and double bonds are formed between adenine and thymine. The geometry of each DNA strand is such that they can only form a double-stranded molecule by being antiparallel, that is, the orientation of one strand is in the 5' to 3' direction, while the complementary strand runs 3' to 5'.

In prokaryotes and eukaryotes, duplication of the genome occurs at replication bubbles, each of which contains two replication forks. The bubbles are regions of the DNA that have dissociated so that daughter strands can be synthesized. A prokaryote chromosome has a single replication bubble, whereas a eukaryote chromosome has many. Consequently, DNA replication in eukaryotes does not begin at one end of the chromosome and continue until it reaches the other end; instead, replication begins at many places simultaneously and progresses until all the bubbles have fused, at which point duplication of the chromosome is complete.

DNA replication requires the coordinated effort of a team of enzymes, led by DNA helicase and primase. The helicase is a remarkable

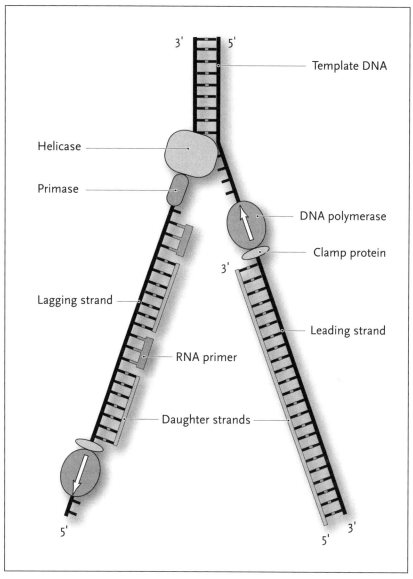

DNA replication. The helicase separates the two strands so the DNA polymerase can synthesize new strands. The primase provides replication signals for the polymerase, in the form of RNA primers, and the clamp protein keeps the polymerase from falling off the DNA. The leading strand requires only a single primer (not shown). The lagging strand requires many primers, and the daughter strand is synthesized as a series of DNA fragments that are later joined into one continuous strand.

enzyme that is responsible for initiating the formation of the bubble and for separating the two DNA strands. This enzyme moves at an astonishing rate, separating 1,000 nucleotides every second. Helicase gets its name from the fact that DNA is a helix, wherein the two strands coil around each other like two strands in a piece of rope. Consequently, helicase is not just separating the two strands but also unwinding them as the replication fork progresses.

The enzyme that is directly responsible for reading the template strand, and for constructing the new daughter strand, is called DNA polymerase. This enzyme reads the parental DNA in the 3' to 5' direction and creates a daughter strand that grows 5' to 3'. DNA polymerase also has an editorial function: It checks the preceding nucleotide to make sure it is correct before it will add a nucleotide to the growing chain. The editor function of this enzyme introduces an interesting problem: How can the polymerase add the very first nucleotide, given that it has to check a preceding nucleotide before adding a new one? A special enzyme called primase, which is attached to the helicase, solves this problem. Primase synthesizes short pieces of RNA that form a DNA-RNA double-stranded region. The RNA becomes a temporary part of the daughter strand, thus priming the DNA polymerase by providing the crucial first nucleotide in the new strand. Once the chromosome is duplicated, DNA repair enzymes remove the RNA primers and replace them with DNA nucleotides.

For every replication fork there is a leading and lagging strand. The leading strand reads 3' to 5' in the direction of the fork, whereas the lagging strand reads 5' to 3'. Since DNA polymerase reads the template 3' to 5', the leading strand only requires a single primer, which is laid down as soon as the replication bubble forms. The lagging strand, however, has to have many primers, and these are laid down as the fork progresses. This is why the helicase and the primase, as shown in the figure on page 65, are located on the lagging strand. DNA polymerase can duplicate the leading strand continuously, in one long piece, whereas the lagging strand has to be duplicated with many discontinuous pieces, from one primer to the next.

This may seem like an awkward solution, but the alternative is to place a single primer at the 3' tips of each strand and then replicate them both continuously. But this would mean that one helicase and one polymerase would have to travel the entire length of each strand. Even with the helicase moving as fast as it does, it would be a very slow way of replicating the genome. Using multiple replication forks per chromosome is analogous to parallel processing, which can dramatically reduce the time it takes to complete a task.

Binary Fission

Prokaryotes all divide by a simple process called binary fission. These cells grow continuously during interphase and the growth is coordinated with the duplication of the chromosome. Soon after the replication bubble forms, one strand of the chromosome is attached to the membrane at one end of the cell, and the other strand is attached to the opposite end. Growth of the cell and the completion of DNA replication are coordinated with the formation of a septum, or invagination, of the cell membrane, which eventually divides the cell into two. The formation of the septum is initiated by a protein called FtsZ, but the details of the process are still unclear.

Mitosis

Cell division among the eukaryotes is more complicated than it is in prokaryotes. The biggest problem eukaryotes have to deal with, compared with prokaryotes, is their enormous genome, spread out over many chromosomes, which must be replicated, packaged, arranged, and sorted before the cell can divide. Division is by a process known as mitosis, which is divided into four stages: prophase, metaphase, anaphase, and telophase. All of these stages are marked out in accordance with the behavior of the nucleus and the chromosomes.

Prophase marks the period during which the duplicated chromosomes begin condensation, and the two centrosomes begin moving to opposite poles of the cell. Under the microscope, the chromosomes become visible as X-shaped structures, which are the two duplicated chromosomes, often called sister chromatids. A special region of each chromosome, called a centromere, holds the chromatids together. Proteins bind to the centromere to form a structure called the kinetochore (see the figure on page 68).

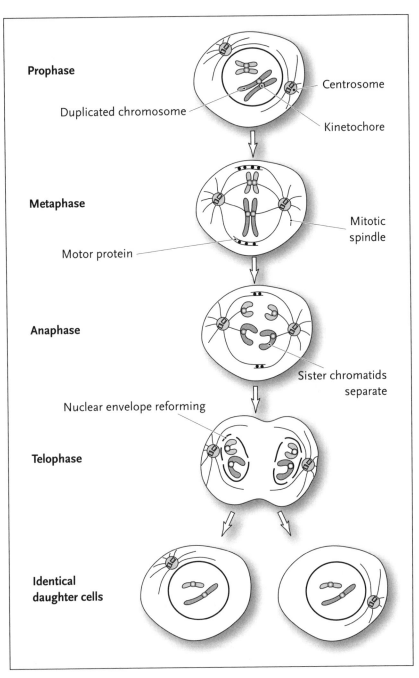

Prophase

Duplicated chromosome

Centrosome

Kinetochore

Metaphase

Mitotic spindle

Motor protein

Anaphase

Sister chromatids separate

Nuclear envelope reforming

Telophase

Identical daughter cells

Mitosis. Principal stages dealing with the movement and partitioning of the chromosomes between the future daughter cells. For clarity, only two chromosomes are shown.

Metaphase is a period during which the chromosomes are sorted out and aligned between the two centrosomes. By this time, the nuclear membrane has completely broken down. The two centrosomes and the microtubules fanning out between them form the mitotic spindle. The area in between the spindles, where the chromosomes are aligned, is often referred to as the metaphase plate. Some of the microtubules make contact with the kinetochores, while others overlap, with motor proteins situated in between (for clarity, only two chromosomes are shown in the figure on page 68). Eukaryotes are normally diploid, so a cell would have two copies of each chromosome, one from the mother and one from the father.

Anaphase is characterized by the movement of the duplicated chromosomes to opposite poles of the cell. The first step is the release of an enzyme that breaks the bonds holding the kinetochores together, thus allowing the sister chromatids to separate from each other while remaining bound to their respective microtubules. Motor proteins then move along the microtubule dragging the chromosomes to opposite ends of the cell. Using energy supplied by ATP, the motor proteins break the microtubule down as it drags the chromosome along so that

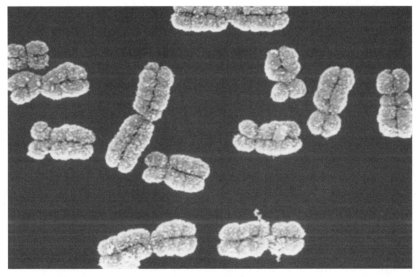

Scanning electron micrograph of human chromosomes in metaphase. (*Courtesy of Biophoto Associates/Photo Researchers, Inc.*)

the microtubule is gone by the time the chromosome reaches the spindle pole. Throughout this process, the motor proteins and the chromosome manage to stay one step ahead of the disintegrating microtubule. The overlapping microtubules aid movement of the chromosomes toward the poles as another type of motor protein pushes the microtubules in opposite directions effectively forcing the centrosomes towards the poles. This accounts for the greater overlap of microtubules in metaphase as compared with anaphase.

During telophase, the daughter chromosomes arrive at the spindle poles and decondense to form the relaxed chromatin characteristic of interphase nuclei. The nuclear envelope begins forming around the chromosomes, marking the end of mitosis. During the same period, a contractile ring, made of the proteins myosin and actin, begins pinching the parental cell in two. This stage, separate from mitosis, is called cytokinesis and leads to the formation of two daughter cells, each with one nucleus.

Meiosis

Unlike mitosis, which leads to the growth of an organism, meiosis is intended for sexual reproduction and occurs exclusively in ovaries and testes. Eukaryotes, being diploid, receive chromosomes from both parents; if gametes were produced using mitosis, a catastrophic growth in the number of chromosomes would occur each time a sperm fertilized an egg. Meiosis is a special form of cell division that produces haploid gametes (eggs and sperm), each possessing half as many chromosomes as the diploid cell. When haploid gametes fuse, they produce an embryo with the correct number of chromosomes.

The existence of meiosis was first suggested 100 years ago when microbiologists counted the number of chromosomes in somatic and germ cells. The roundworm, for example, was found to have four chromosomes in its somatic cells but only two in its gametes. Many other studies also compared the amount of DNA in nuclei from somatic cells and gonads, always with the same result: The amount of DNA in somatic cells is exactly double the amount in fully mature gametes.

To understand how this could be, scientists studied cell division in the gonads and were able to show that meiosis occurs as two rounds of cell

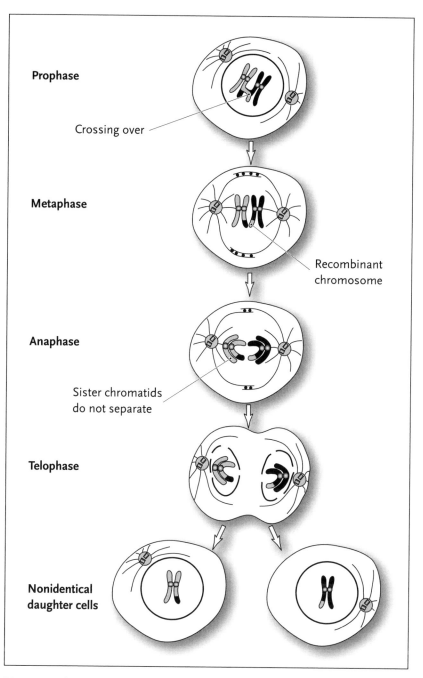

Prophase

Crossing over

Metaphase

Recombinant
chromosome

Anaphase

Sister chromatids
do not separate

Telophase

**Nonidentical
daughter cells**

Meiosis I. The most notable features include genetic recombination (crossing over) between the homologous chromosomes during prophase, comigration of the sister chromatids during anaphase, and the production of nonidentical daughter cells. Only one homologous pair is shown.

division with only one round of DNA synthesis. The two rounds of division were called meiosis I and meiosis II, and scientists observed that both could be divided into the same four stages known to occur in mitosis. Indeed, meiosis II is virtually identical to a mitotic division. Meiosis I resembles mitosis, but close examination shows three important differences: gene swapping occurs between homologous chromosomes in prophase; homologs (i.e., two homologous chromosomes) remain paired at metaphase, instead of lining up at the plate as is done in mitosis; and the kinetochores do not separate at anaphase.

Homologous chromosomes are two identical chromosomes that come from different parents. For example, humans have 23 chromosomes from the father and the same 23 from the mother. We each have a maternal chromosome 1 and a paternal chromosome 1; they carry the same genes but specify slightly different traits. Chromosome 1 may carry the gene for eye color, but the maternal version, or allele, may specify blue eyes, whereas the paternal allele specifies brown. During prophase, homologous pairs exchange large numbers of genes by swapping whole pieces of chromosome. Thus one of the maternal chromotids (gray in the figure on page 71) ends up with a piece of paternal chromosome, and a paternal chromatid receives the corresponding piece of maternal chromosome. Mixing genetic material in this way is unique to meiosis, and it is one of the reasons sexual reproduction has been such a powerful evolutionary force.

During anaphase of meiosis I, the kinetochores do not separate as they do in mitosis. The effect of this is to separate the maternal and paternal chromosomes by sending them to different daughter cells, although the segregation is random. That is, the daughter cells receive a random assortment of maternal and paternal chromosomes, rather than one daughter cell receiving all paternal chromosomes and the other all maternal chromosomes. Random segregation, along with genetic recombination, accounts for the fact that while children resemble their parents, they do not look or act exactly like them. These two mechanisms are responsible for the remarkable adaptability of all eukaryotes.

Meiosis II begins immediately after the completion of meiosis I, which produces two daughter cells, each containing a duplicated parental chromosome and a recombinant chromosome consisting of both paternal and maternal DNA. These two cells divide mitotically to produce four haploid cells, each of which is genetically unique, containing unaltered or recombinant maternal and paternal chromosomes. This example follows the fate of a single homologous pair. In reality, the four haploid cells, if human, would contain 23 chromosomes each,

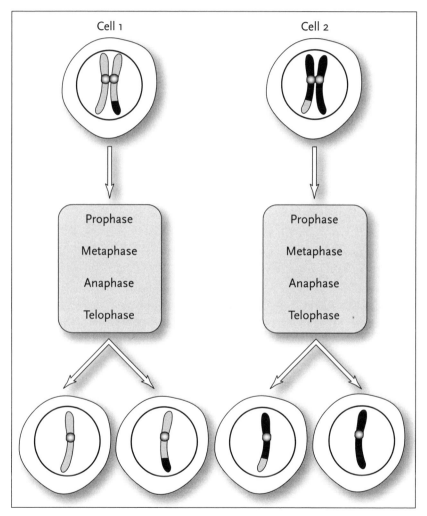

Meiosis II. Cells 1 and 2 were produced in meiosis I. These cells divide mitotically, but without replication of the chromosomes, to produce four genetically unique haploid gametes.

some from the mother, some from the father, some remixed (recombinant), others unaltered.

Meiosis produces haploid cells by passing through two rounds of cell division with only one round of DNA synthesis. However, as we have seen, the process is not just concerned with reducing the number of chromosomes but is also involved in stirring up the genetic pot in order to produce unique gametes that may someday give rise to an equally unique individual.

·5·
GENES

Genes are a precious biological commodity: They hold the key to a cell's survival and are the summation of countless natural experiments over millions of years of evolution. Nature has poked, prodded, modified, and tweaked each gene, almost to exhaustion. Those that fail the test, or do not live up to expectations, are eliminated. The genes that we find today, in ourselves and in other organisms, are the survivors. The elaborate codes they carry, and the proteins or RNA molecules they specify, produce organisms that are also survivors: hardy creatures that are resourceful, diligent, and well adapted to their environment.

The attention nature pays to a gene is analogous to the labors of an artist, who spends many hours carefully shaping, carving, and polishing a sculpture. Work on the sculpture may last for weeks or years and often goes through many revisions, each of which brings the object closer to the artist's vision. The difference between the artist and nature is that nature works on its sculptures indirectly, by polishing or altering genes; removing a base here, adding one there, and seeing what happens. In many cases, nature is never satisfied with the outcome, and so the gene, and its product, continues changing over time. Sometimes, however, nature seems to hit it right, and the gene remains unchanged for millions of years.

These and many other insights into the nature of the gene have been hard-won, over many years, by thousands of researchers studying different species of plant and animal life. But the pace of this kind of work increased dramatically throughout the late 1990s with the initiation of the human genome project. The final draft of the human genome was completed in 2003 and provides a wealth of information regarding the structure, organization, and evolution of our genes.

The Human Genome Project

Sequencing the entire human genome is an idea that grew over a period of 20 years, beginning in the early 1980s. At that time, the DNA sequencing method invented by the British biochemist Fred Sanger, then at the University of Cambridge, was but a few years old and had only been used to sequence viral or mitochondrial genomes (see chapter 8 for a description of sequencing methods). Indeed, one of the first genomes to be sequenced was that of bacteriophage G4, a virus that infects the bacterium *Escherichia coli (E. coli)*. The G4 genome consists of 5,577 nucleotide pairs (or base pairs, abbreviated bp) and was sequenced in Dr. Sanger's laboratory in 1979. By 1982, the Sanger protocol was used by others to sequence the genome of the animal virus SV40 (5,224 bp), the human mitochondrion (16,569 bp), and bacteriophage lambda (48,502 bp). Besides providing invaluable data, these projects demonstrated the feasibility of sequencing very large genomes.

The possibility of sequencing the entire human genome was first discussed at scientific meetings organized by the United States Department of Energy (DOE) between 1984 and 1986. A committee appointed by the U.S. National Research Council endorsed the idea in 1988 but recommended a broader program to include the sequencing of the genes of humans, bacteria, yeast, worms, flies, and mice. They also called for the establishment of research programs devoted to the ethical, legal, and social issues raised by human genome research. The program was formally launched in late 1990 as a consortium consisting of coordinated sequencing projects in the United States, Britain, France, Germany, Japan, and China. At about the same time, the Human Genome Organization (HUGO) was founded to provide a forum for international coordination of genomic research.

By 1995, the consortium had established a strategy, called hierarchical shotgun sequencing, which they applied to the human genome as well as to the other organisms mentioned. With this strategy, genomic DNA is cut into one-megabase (Mb) fragments (i.e., each fragment consists of 1 million bases) that are cloned into bacterial artificial

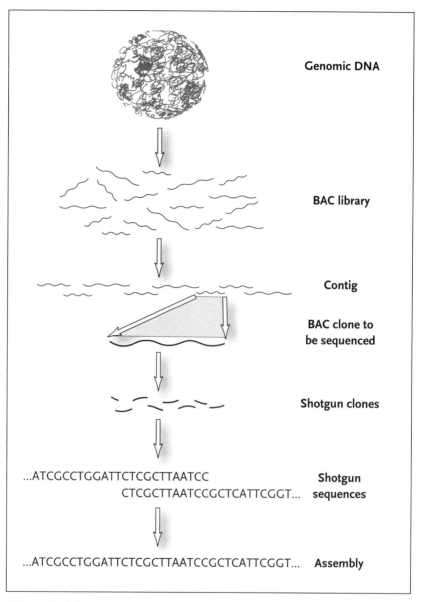

Hierarchical shotgun sequencing. Total genomic DNA is cut with a restriction enzyme into one-megabase fragments (i.e., 1 million base pairs per fragment) that are cloned into bacterial artificial chromosomes (BACs) to form a library. The BAC fragments are partially characterized in order to organize them into an overlapping assembly called a contig. Clones are selected from the contigs for shotgun sequencing and final assembly.

chromosomes (BACs) to form a library of DNA fragments. The BAC fragments are partially characterized, then organized into an overlapping assembly called a contig. Clones are selected from the contigs for shotgun sequencing. That is, each shotgun clone is digested into small 1,000 bp fragments, sequenced, and then assembled into the final sequence with the aid of computers. Organizing the initial BAC fragments into contigs greatly simplifies the final assembly stage.

Sequencing of the human genome was divided into two stages. The first stage, completed in 2001, was a rough draft that covered about 80 percent of the genome with an estimated size of more than 3 billion bases (also expressed as 3 gigabases, or 3 Gb). The final draft, completed in April 2003, covers the entire genome and refines the data for areas of the genome that were difficult to sequence. It also filled in many gaps that occurred in the rough draft. The final draft of the human genome gives us a great deal of information that may be divided into three categories: gene content, gene origins, and gene organization.

GENE CONTENT   Analysis of the final draft has shown that the human genome consists of 3.2 Gb of DNA, that encodes about 30,000 genes (estimates range between 25,000 to 32,000). The estimated number of genes is surprisingly low; many scientists had believed the human genome contained 100,000 genes. By comparison, the fruit fly has 13,338 genes, and the simple roundworm, *Caenorhabditis elegans* (*C. elegans*), has 18,266. The genome data suggests that human complexity, as compared to the fruit fly or the worm, is not simply due to the absolute number of genes but also involves the complexity of the proteins that are encoded by those genes. In general, human proteins tend to be much more complex than those of lower organisms. Data from the final draft and other sources provides a detailed overview of the functional profile of human cellular proteins (see table on page 79).

GENE ORIGINS   Fully one half of human genes originated as transposable elements, also known as jumping genes (these will be discussed at length in a following section). Equally surprising is the fact that 220 of our genes were obtained by horizontal transfer from bacteria, rather than ancestral, or vertical, inheritance. In other words, we obtained these genes directly from bacteria, probably during

FUNCTIONAL PROFILE OF
KNOWN CELLULAR PROTEINS

Process	Number of Proteins
Energy metabolism	5,200
DNA replication/repair	900
Transcription/translation	3,200
Signaling (intra- and extra-cellular)	3,100
Protein modifiers	850
Transport	1,200
Multifunctional proteins	400
Structural	900
Defense	1,050
Total	**16,800***

*The total shown is about half of the estimated 32,000 protein encoding genes in the human genome. The discrepancy is due to the fact that many genes have an unknown function.

episodes of infection, in a kind of natural gene therapy, or gene swapping. We know this to be the case because, while these genes occur in bacteria, they are not present in yeast, fruit flies, or any other eukaryotes that have been tested.

The function of most of the horizontally transferred genes is unclear, although a few may code for basic metabolic enzymes. A notable exception is a gene that codes for an enzyme called monoamine oxidase (MAO). Monoamines are neurotransmitters, such as dopamine, norepinephrine, and serotonin, which are needed for neural signaling in the human central nervous system. Monoamine oxidase plays a crucial role in the turnover of these neurotransmitters (see chapter 6). How MAO, obtained from bacteria, could have developed such an important role in human physiology is a great mystery.

GENE ORGANIZATION   In prokaryotes, genes are simply arranged in tandem along the chromosome, with little if any DNA separating one gene from the other. Each gene is transcribed into messenger RNA (mRNA), which is translated into protein. Indeed, in prokaryotes, which

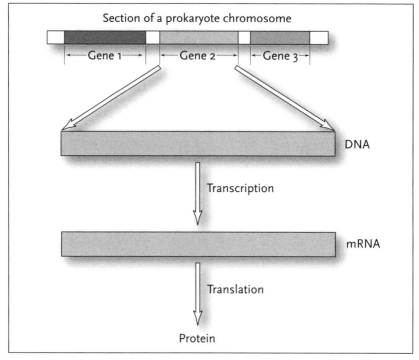

Prokaryote genes. The genes are arranged in tandem along the chromosome with little, if any, DNA separating one gene from the other. The genes may code for protein, as shown above for Gene 2, or ribosomal RNA (rRNA).

have no nucleus, translation often begins even before transcription is complete. In eukaryotes, as we might expect, gene organization is more complex. Data from the genome project shows clearly that eukaryote genes are split into subunits, called exons, and that each exon is separated by a length of DNA, called an intron. A gene, consisting of introns and exons, is separated from other genes by long stretches of noncoding DNA called intervening sequences. Eukaryote genes are transcribed into a primary RNA molecule that includes exon and intron sequences. The primary transcript never leaves the nucleus and is never translated into protein. Nuclear enzymes remove the introns from the primary transcript, after which the exons are joined together to form the mature mRNA. Thus only the exons carry the necessary code to produce a protein.

Why do eukaryotes, all of which have split genes, go through such a laborious procedure when the simple and direct method used by prokaryotes works so well and seems so eloquent? The answer lies with

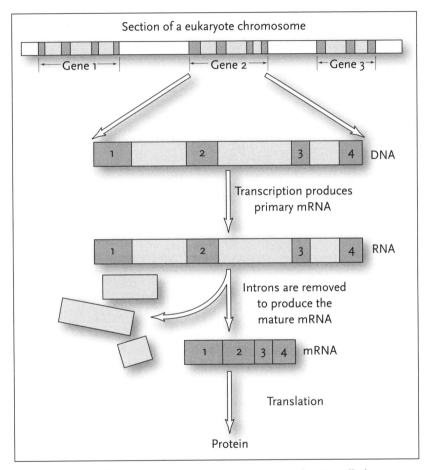

Eukaryote genes. The genes are arranged in separate subunits called exons (dark gray) and introns (light gray). Each gene, which consists of introns and exons, is separated from other genes by long stretches of noncoding DNA called intervening sequences (white areas). The genes are transcribed into a primary RNA molecule that includes exon and intron sequences. Nuclear enzymes remove the introns from the primary transcript, and then the exons are joined together to form the mature mRNA, which is translated into protein. Transcription of ribosomal genes is similar, except that the exons become the individual rRNAs.

the need to maximize protein evolution and to protect the genome from insertional mutagenesis. The rate at which proteins evolve can be maximized by a process known as exon shuffling. Any given protein usually has more than one job that it is good at. One end of a protein may be good at binding to a specific region of the genome, while the other end specializes in phosphorylating other proteins. The middle region of the protein may give it a special corkscrew shape. If each of these regions is encoded by three different exons, then it is easy to see how new proteins could emerge very quickly by recombining, or shuffling, preexisting exons.

Insertional mutagenesis occurs because our world is full of viruses that can infect eukaryote cells. The life cycle of many of these viruses is such that they are able to insert their genome into a chromosome of the

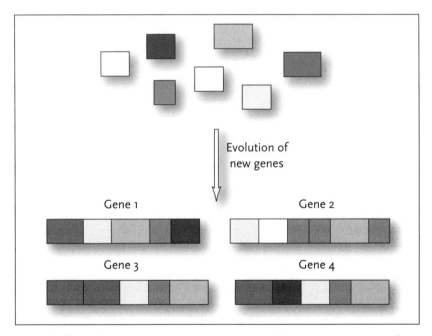

Exon shuffling. New eukaryote genes can evolve without the appearance of new mutations simply by recombining, or shuffling, preexisting exons. In the example shown, seven exons were used to produce four novel genes, each of which would code for a novel protein. Exon shuffling is not possible in a prokaryote genome.

host cell. If eukaryotes had a simple prokaryote-like genome, then no matter where the virus inserted, it would likely destroy, damage, or mutate a gene. On the other hand, the eukaryote genome contains large regions of noncoding DNA (introns and intervening sequences) so that, in all probability, insertion of a virus will not damage any of the genes. The only way a virus can damage any of our genes is if it happens to insert at an exon-intron boundary. If this happens, special DNA sequences located at the boundary are corrupted, leading to the production of defective messenger RNA.

The fact is that human genes and the genes of most eukaryotes are hidden in a sea of noncoding DNA. As already mentioned, the human genome consists of 3.2 Gb of DNA and contains about 30,000 genes. With an average gene size of 1,200 bp (based on exons only), this amounts to a total of 36 Mb of coding DNA, or roughly 1.0 percent of the total DNA content. The vast majority of our DNA codes for nothing but has a crucial role in protecting our genes from marauding pieces of DNA.

The Future of Genomic Research

The many insights into the structure, evolution, and organization of our genes that the genome project has provided are expected to revolutionize the study of many medical disorders. Various research communities, as diverse as nursing, psychiatry, and gene therapy, have already written summary articles outlining the many advances they expect to make with the available sequence data. Cancer research provides the most striking example of the impact this data has already had. Scientists at the Sanger Institute in Cambridge, England, established a research program in 2001 to use human sequence data to identify all cancer-causing genes in the human genome. Within a few months they were able to isolate and fully characterize a gene that causes more than 70 percent of all malignant melanomas. Their analysis is so complete and so illuminating that they believe a cure for this deadly form of cancer will be available within a few years, and they expect to complete the identification of all other cancer genes by 2005. Cancer is only one of many prominent genetic diseases. Similar advances are expected in the discovery and characterization of genes that cause neurological disorders, cardiovascular disease, diabetes, metabolic disorders, and aging.

Turning Genes On and Off

All genes come equipped with a controlling region, called the promoter, that serves the same function as a light switch and provides the binding site for the RNA polymerase that transcribes the gene into RNA. The switching function of the promoter is regulated by other proteins, known generally as transcription factors, that bind to the promoter in a way that either blocks the polymerase (the "off" position) or activates it (the "on" position). In some cases, two or more genes are controlled by the same promoter, so when the promoter switches on, all the genes are activated simultaneously (i.e., transcribed into RNA). This arrangement, in which a single promoter is linked to two or more genes, is known as an operon, and it is very common among prokaryotes. Indeed, it was the study of the bacterial *Lac* operon that gave geneticists their first insights into the control of gene expression. The *Lac* operon has three structural genes that code for proteins needed for the import and processing of the sugar lactose, from which this operon gets its name. By convention, these genes are known as *z, y,* and *a*. The *z* gene codes for β-galactosidase, an enzyme that hydrolyzes lactose to galactose and glucose. The *y* gene codes for a permease, which facilitates the entry of lactose into the bacteria, and the *a* gene codes for a transacetylase, which metabolizes lactoselike compounds.

A simplified scheme for controlling the *Lac* operon is shown in the figure on page 85. A repressor protein binds to the promoter, in a region called the operator, thus preventing the binding of the polymerase. This happens whenever glucose, the preferred sugar, is available. As long as the repressor is bound to the operator, the operon is turned off. Depletion of glucose stimulates the binding of a protein called catabolite activator protein (CAP) to another area of the promoter, called the regulator, or CAP site. If lactose happens to be present when the glucose is depleted, the repressor is forced off the promoter, allowing the binding of the polymerase. Once bound, CAP activates the polymerase and the *Lac* operon is transcribed.

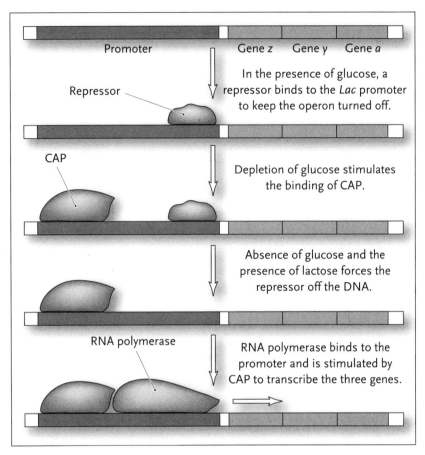

The Lac operon. This operon consists of three structural genes (z, y, and a) under the control of a single promoter. The repressor binds to a portion of the promoter, called the operator. The catabolite activator protein (CAP) binds at the opposite end of the promoter, in a region known as the regulator, or CAP site. The Lac operon is designed to stay off as long as glucose is present.

The control of gene expression in eukaryotes is more complex, but the basic logic remains the same. In this case, control occurs in three steps. First, special proteins expose the gene's promoter; second, transcription factors assemble on the promoter; and third, regulatory proteins activate the transcriptional machinery. Eukaryote regulatory proteins belong to three families represented by helix-loop-helix, zinc finger, and leucine zipper proteins. The various members of these families are able to

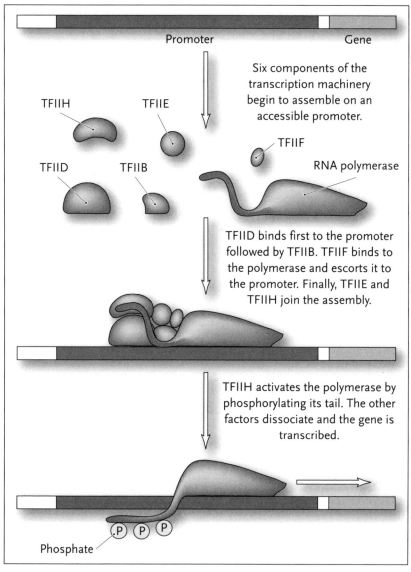

The control of eukaryote gene expression. RNA polymerase and five transcription factors assemble on an exposed promoter. Once these components are in place, transcription factor IIH (TFIIH) is activated by a eukaryote-specific enhancer, analogous to the prokaryote CAP. In this case, the enhancer is located some distance—sometimes thousands of base pairs—upstream (i.e., to the left) from the polymerase. Only a portion of the gene is shown.

recognize specific DNA sequences that are associated with the promoter of every gene. The interaction between the regulatory protein and the DNA is not passive. Rather than simply binding to the DNA, the protein changes the conformation of the local neighborhood by twisting the DNA into a more opened helical structure. The conformational change that the DNA undergoes exposes the promoter to the transcription machinery. This process is complex and not fully understood, but is known to involve a relaxation of the DNA helix as well as alterations to the local chromatin conformation.

After the promoter is exposed, six components of the transcription machinery, including RNA polymerase and five transcription factors, quickly assemble. Once the transcription machinery is assembled, the regulatory protein activates a transcription factor, called IIH, which in turn activates the polymerase to permit transcription of the gene.

For a prokaryote, the decision to turn a particular gene on or off is relatively straightforward, and usually involves signals that it receives directly from the environment. If we could read the mind of a bacterium, its thought processes might go something like this:

> Is there any glucose around? If not, is there any lactose? If there is plenty of glucose on hand, keep the Lac operon off, because there is no point in running it otherwise. If we run out of glucose but detect lactose, turn the glucose operon off and the Lac operon on. If we run out of glucose and lactose, activate auxiliary operons that are capable of processing other sugars, such as maltose or arabinose. If there are no sugars around, activate the genes responsible for processing proteins, fats, and anything else that carries calories.

The control of gene expression in eukaryotes generally adheres to the logic established by the prokaryotes. However, in eukaryotes, the details of the process are more involved, requiring a greater number of steps and molecular participants. Eukaryotes are much more careful about controlling spurious and inappropriate gene expression. This is particularly true for multicellular eukaryotes, for which sloppy control of gene expression can lead to cancerous growths. The desire for precise control can be seen in the number of factors that are needed just to establish a transcription crew in eukaryotes as opposed to prokaryotes (see figure on page 86). A process that has many components automatically provides many pathways for controlling that process. This is critical for multicellular eukaryotes, all of which are absolutely dependent on careful regulation of gene expression.

Gene Monitors and Repair Crews

DNA is a very stable molecule, but it is not immutable. Every day, in a typical human cell, thousands of nucleotides are being damaged by spontaneous chemical events, environmental pollutants, and radiation. In many cases, it takes only a single defective nucleotide within the coding region of a gene to produce an inactive, mutant protein. The most common forms of DNA damage are depurination and deamination. Depurination is the loss of a purine base (guanine or adenine) resulting in a gap in the DNA sequence, referred to as a "missing tooth." Deamination converts cytosine to uracil, a base that is normally found only in RNA.

It has been estimated that about 5,000 purines are lost from each human cell every day, and that over the same time period, 100 cytosines are deaminated per cell. Depurination and deamination produce a great deal of damage, and in either case, the daughter strand ends up with a missing nucleotide, and possibly a mutated gene, as the DNA replication machinery simply bypasses the uracil or the missing tooth. If left unrepaired, the mutated genes will be passed on to all daughter cells, with catastrophic consequences for the organism as a whole.

DNA damage caused by depurination is repaired by special nuclear proteins that detect the missing tooth, excise about 10 nucleotides on either side of the damage, and then, using the complementary strand as a guide, reconstruct the strand correctly. Deamination is dealt with by a remarkable group of DNA repair enzymes known as base-flippers. These enzymes monitor the DNA one nucleotide at a time. After binding to a nucleotide, a base-flipper breaks the hydrogen bonds holding the nucleotide to its complementary partner. It then performs the maneuver for which it gets its name. Holding on to the nucleotide, it rotates the base a full 360 degrees, inspects it carefully, and, if it detects any damage, cuts the base out and discards it. In this case, the base-flipper leaves the final repair to the missing-tooth crew that detects and repairs the gap as described previously. If the nucleotide is normal, the base-flipper rotates it back into place and reseals the hydrogen bonds.

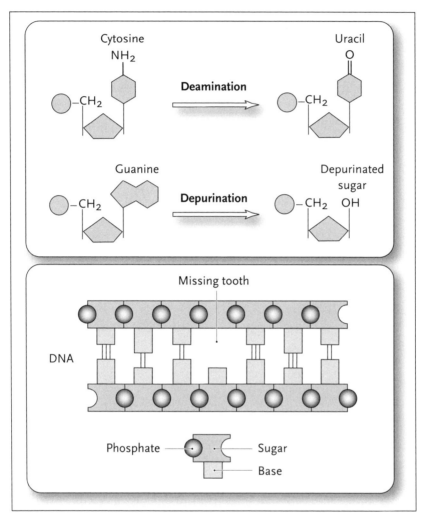

DNA damage from deamination and depurination. Deamination, or loss of an amino group (NH2), converts cytosine to uracil. Depurination results in the loss of a purine nucleotide (top panel), leaving a gap, or "missing tooth," in the DNA molecule (bottom panel). Both types of damage can lead to a catastrophic buildup of mutations if not repaired.

Base-flippers and the missing-tooth crew work 24 hours a day, seven days a week. Scientists have estimated that these crews inspect and repair the entire genome of a typical human cell in less than 24 hours.

Jumping Genes

When first proposed by the American geneticist Barbara McClintock in 1951, the idea that genes could move, or jump, from one location in the genome to some other location was greeted with disbelief and disdain. For more than 20 years, this idea languished in a kind of scientific limbo until the advent of recombinant technology made it possible to prove the existence of these wandering genes, formally known as transposons or transposable elements. By the 1980s, McClintock's work was finally given the recognition it deserved, and in 1983, at the age of 81, she was awarded the Nobel Prize in medicine. She died on September 2, 1992.

McClintock's work provided several insights into the organization and evolution of the eukaryote genome: First, the position of some genes, within the genome, is flexible; second, the roles of transposable elements, introns, and intervening sequences are interconnected; and third, viruses are direct descendents of jumping genes. With the completion of the genome project, we now know that many of our genes were once transposable elements, including the 220 genes obtained by horizontal transfer from bacteria.

Insertional mutagenesis, discussed earlier in the chapter, is the connection between a jumping gene and an intervening sequence. As mentioned, only 1.0 percent of the human genome contains genes, with the rest of the DNA consisting of intervening sequences and introns. Our genome has evolved into a form that accommodates mobile genes. In such a genome, the odds of a transposable element damaging an existing gene are extremely small. When a jumping gene moves, it will, in all likelihood, reinsert into an intervening sequence, a region that lacks genes, where it may stay for thousands or millions of years. After having been duplicated, most transposons move again, thus producing many copies of the same gene, which are sprinkled around the genome. These copies of the original gene are then free to mutate into other genes that may eventually become useful to the organism. Thus copies of the original transposon are the source of many of the genes now present in the human genome.

The flexibility of a transposable genome is perhaps the single most important characteristic that led to the explosive adaptability of eukaryotes and the many life forms, especially the multicellular creatures, they produced. Such a genome is also important to modern medical thera-pies, such as gene therapy, which attempts to cure a disease by introduc-ing a normal gene into the patient's genome. If our genome were organized like that of the prokaryotes, such a therapy would be nearly impossible.

Transposable elements have given us a flexible and extremely pow-erful genomic organization, but they have also given us the viruses and all the illnesses they produce, such as AIDS, polio, and the common cold. Somehow, millions of years ago, a jumping gene learned how to jump right out of the cell. It acquired this ability in small steps as it moved from one place in the genome to another. A jumping gene that moves usually reinserts into an intervening sequence, devoid of other genes; occasionally, a transposon reinserts next to a gene, possibly one that codes for a protein that could serve as a capsid, a protein that pro-tects a virus's genome, and forms the overall structure of the viral par-ticle. The next time such a transposon moved, it would take a copy of the potential capsid gene with it. Eventually, by moving from place to place, the transposon would have collected a large number of genes that not only made it possible for it to escape from the cell but also gave it the power to reinfect other cells. When that happened, a simple mobile genetic element went from being a molecular curiosity to a living thing, equipped with a life cycle and the power of reproduction.

.6.

FROM CELLS TO BODIES

Eukaryotes seem to have been destined for multicellularity. Not that they fared poorly as single cells; quite to the contrary, the phylogenetic class protista is one of the most successful and diverse groups of organisms around. But becoming multicellular requires a complex communication network backed up by far more genes and proteins than a prokaryote can muster. Prokaryotes did, however, lay the groundwork and formed the first, though temporary, association of cells in the form of fruiting bodies containing the spores of many individual cells.

The Road to Multicellular Creatures

Myxobacteria, discussed in chapter 2, were the first cells to form brief multicellular associations for the purpose of reproduction. These prokaryotes spend most of their time as free-living vegetative cells. Starvation is the trigger that leads to the aggregation of these cells into a sporulating fruiting body. As spores, the cells can hibernate until conditions improve, and in addition, wind currents may carry them to other, more favorable locations, where they can germinate with the hope of finding food. This type of multicellular colonial behavior was refined by eukaryotes such as the amoeba *Dictyostelium discoideum* and the green algae *Volvox.* Colonial forms eventually gave rise to true multicellular organisms such as sea sponges and sea cucumbers, followed by higher organisms, both aquatic and terrestrial (see table on page 93).

Dictyostelium, a social amoeba that feeds on bacteria among the leaf litter of forest floors, is the eukaryote version of the myxobacterial life cycle. In this case, the formation of the fruiting body is preceded by the

PROGRESSIVE STAGES OF MULTICELLULARITY

Stage	Description
Cellular slugs	Temporary associations of identical cells, cooperating for a common purpose. The only known example among eukaryotes is *Dictyostelium*.
Cellular colonies	Permanent associations among identical cells. The colonies are capable of producing gametes (sperm and eggs). Two examples are *Gonium* and *Volvox*.
Sponges	Aquatic creatures constructed from different types of cells, including gametes, that differentiate during development. The cells are not organized into tissues and there is no nervous system.
Cnidarians	Aquatic creatures that include the jellyfish, sea anemones, hydroids, and corals. In these organisms are the first appearance of tissues, a rudimentary nervous system, a mouth, and digestive tract. These animals are constructed from only eight cell types: epithelial, muscle, neural, glandular, interstitial, gonadal, mesenchyme, and the cnidoblast, or stinging cell.
Mollusks	Organisms that include clams, octopoids, and snails, some of which are terrestrial. These animals have a well-developed mouth and digestive tract. In addition, some, like the octopus, have a highly developed central nervous system.
Echinoderms	Aquatic animals that include sea stars, sea urchins, and sea cucumbers. All have well-developed tissues, including a digestive tract and nervous system.
Cartilaginous fish	Fish having a full set of organs and tissues but lacking a true skeleton. This group includes sharks and rays.
Vertebrates	A subphylum of animals found in the water, on land, and in the air. They include bony fishes, amphibians, reptiles, birds, and mammals. Organs and tissue systems are refined to an extraordinary degree, allowing reptiles, birds, and mammals to colonize the land.

formation of a migrating slug, consisting of thousands of individual *Dictyostelium* cells. It is the slug phase that distinguishes this life cycle from that of the myxobacteria. The slug behaves like a single entity with a common purpose. It moves among the leaf litter as though it were a real slug or worm, testing the environment for a suitable place to form a fruiting body. Usually, the slug tries to migrate as far above the leaf litter as possible. In this way, the fruiting body gets maximum exposure to

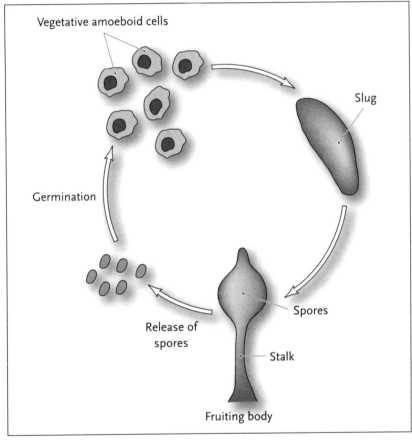

Life cycle of *Dictyostelium*. Vegetative amoeboid cells feed on bacteria in the soil. When food runs low, the cells aggregate to form a migrating slug eventually transformed into a fruiting body containing spores. Air currents spread the spores to new locations, and if conditions are favorable, the spores germinate into vegetative cells.

wind currents, thus improving the chance that the spores will be carried to a new location.

As with myxobacteria, the main stimulus for slug formation is starvation. When the individual cells run out of food, they release a chemical called cyclic adenosine monophosphate (cAMP) that serves as a call for all the *Dictyostelium* cells in the immediate neighborhood to aggregate. The hungriest cells answer the call first, forming the headend of the slug. The not-so-hungry cells also answer the call, but they take their time in getting there. As a consequence, arriving late, they form the posterior of the slug. When the slug finds a suitable location, the anterior portion anchors to the substratum, and all the cells in this region form the stalk, while the cells at the posterior form the spores. The cells forming the stalk are doomed; they die soon after the fruiting body is formed. There is an interesting logic associated with this arrangement. Stalk cells are the hungry ones, and therefore they do not have the reserves necessary to make viable spores. The hungry cells, in effect, are being sacrificed for the good of the community as a whole. It is also interesting to note that this early form of multicellularity is associated with such complex behavior and the principle of cooperation for the good of the community.

The green algae, represented by *Gonium* and *Volvox,* produced the first permanent cellular colonies. *Gonium* colonies are small, concave discs, consisting of about 32 cells, whereas *Volvox,* resembling a green glass ball, has up to 50,000 cells. *Volvox* colonies have cytoplasmic bridges that connect the cells together, allowing them to communicate with each other and to share nutrients. Each *Volvox* cell has a single flagellum, the beating of which is coordinated to propel the entire colony through the water like a rolling ball. The various cells within the colony seem to have specialized functions, as they cannot survive if the colony is disrupted. A small number of the cells are specialized for reproduction and serve as precursors for new colonies.

Although *Volvox* cells appear to be specialized, they are all essentially the same kind of cell, looking very much like *Chlamydomonas,* the unicellular green algae that is believed to have given rise to the colonial forms. The next stage in the development of multicellularity came with the appearance of the sea sponges, animals that are constructed from several distinct cell types. These simple animals produce gametes that fuse to form an embryo. Development of the embryo is associated with cellular differentiation by mechanisms that have been retained by higher animals. Sponges, though multicellular, do not have tissues or a nervous system.

A true nervous system made its first appearance with the evolution of the cnidarians (e.g., jellyfish and corals), animals that are made from only eight cell types but which possess a mouth, digestive tract, and tissues, such as epithelia and muscles. These tissues and organ systems were refined by the mollusks (snails and octopods) and echinoderms (sea stars and cucumbers), reaching an exquisite level of sophistication with the appearance of the vertebrates.

Cell Junctions

A *Volvox* colony is held together with simple cytoplasmic bridges. True multicellular creatures have evolved more sophisticated structures, called cell junctions, for holding the tissues and organs together. Three of the most important of these are tight junctions, desmosomes, and gap junctions.

TIGHT JUNCTIONS   These junctions, found primarily in the epithelial lining of an animal's digestive tract, stitch two cells together so tightly that the intercellular space, at the site of the junction, is obliterated. This junction not only keeps the cells together but also performs a very important secondary function of blocking the movement of bacteria and small molecules from the lumen (interior) of the gut into the intercellular space. In other words, tight junctions make the gut leak-proof. Nutrients obtained from the food we eat must pass through the gut's epithelial lining, where they are screened before being allowed to enter general circulation. Without the tight junctions, unwanted chemicals, possibly of a toxic nature, would be absorbed. In addition, the millions of bacteria that inhabit an animal's intestinal tract would quickly spread throughout the body, leading to a fatal infection.

DESMOSOMES   Most of the cells in an animal's body are held together by desmosomes, junctions that are like tiny organic rivets. A protein plaque, analogous to a rivet head, is located beneath the

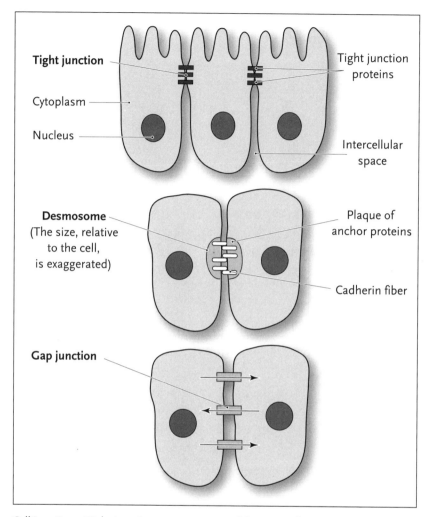

Cell junctions. Tight junctions are constructed from membrane proteins that stitch the two cells together very tightly. Desmosomes, constructed from plaques and protein fibers called cadherins, hold the cells together but allow material to pass through the intercellular space. The gap junction is a hollow tube formed from six identical proteins called connexins (not shown). These junctions hold the cells together while allowing small molecules to pass freely between the cells, as indicated by the arrows. The "gap" refers to the large intercellular space.

membranes of adjacent cells. Another protein, called cadherin, projects from the plaques into the intercellular space where they form chemical bonds with each other, thus holding the two cells together. This junction is more relaxed than a tight junction, and molecules are free to diffuse throughout the intercellular space.

GAP JUNCTIONS   Cells need to be anchored to each other. In many cases, they also need to exchange fluids. The cytoplasmic bridges found in *Volvox* serve both these functions. Gap junctions, consisting primarily of hollow protein tubes, provide both an anchor and a fluid conduit in higher organisms. The sharing of cytoplasm is especially important in cardiac muscle, where the contraction of each myocyte is coordinated by the movement of ions through gap junctions.

Cells in the Human Body

The evolution of multicellular creatures was accompanied by the diversification of cell types. The simplest multicellular animals, such as the sponges and cnidarians, are made from fewer than a dozen cell types, whereas humans are constructed from more than 200 different kinds of cells. These cells represent four primary tissues: epithelium, connective tissue, muscle, and nervous tissue. The primary tissues give rise to all the organs and fluids of the body. For example, epithelium produces skin, gut, glands, and hair, whereas connective tissue gives rise to fibroblasts, bone, blood, and fat cells. Each of the primary tissues is constructed from many different cell types. Based on cell variety alone, the most complex primary tissue is neural, consisting of more than 100 different kinds of neurons.

The many kinds of cells that make up an animal's body differ both in structure and function. This is not to say that a muscle cell, for example, contains organelles different from a neuron or liver cell; these cells are all eukaryotes and therefore have the same basic composition as shown previously. However, the external shape, the number of organelles, and even the DNA content vary widely among the differing cell types. To illustrate the extraordinary variety of cells that make up the human body, this section will describe examples of epithelium and muscle. Examples of connective tissue (cells of the immune system) will be described in the next section, while nervous tissue (neurons) is covered in the following chapter.

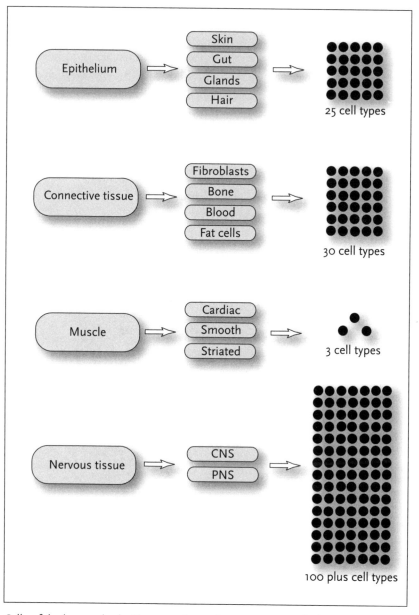

Cells of the human body. There are four primary tissues in the body: epithelium, connective tissue, muscle tissue, and neural tissue. These tissues, representing more than 200 cell types, give rise to the body's structures, blood, and other fluids. The greatest diversity of cell types is found among the tissues of the central nervous system (CNS) and peripheral nervous system (PNS).

EPITHELIUM

Our skin, made from epithelial cells, protects us from dehydration and microbial infections. It also contains sweat glands to help cool the body, sebaceous glands that oil the skin, and hair follicles. The barrier against microbes is produced by ion pumps, located in the membranes of every epithelial cell, that deposit hydrogen ions on the surface of the skin, producing an acid mantle capable of inhibiting the growth of most bacteria. Human epidermis is a stratified epithelium that consists of two populations of squamous cells: the outermost enucleated squames and

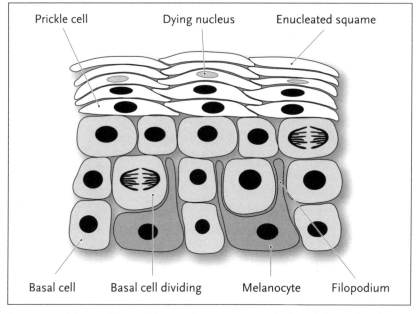

Structure of the epidermis. The epidermis is a stratified epithelium that forms the outer layer of the skin. It consists of three cell populations: squamous cells (the enucleated squames and the prickle cells), the cuboidal basal cells, and at the deepest layers, pigment-containing melanocytes. The basal and squamous cell layers are in a constant state of change. Division of a basal cell is followed by keratinization, a process by which the daughter cells are transformed into prickle cells. Keratin is a tough protein that makes the outer cell layer resistant to abrasion. In the final stage of keratinization, the prickle cell loses its nucleus. The now dead and fully keratinized squame eventually flakes off from the surface. Keratinized squames from the scalp are called dandruff.

the nucleated prickle cells. Just beneath the squamous cells are the cuboidal basal cells, and at the deepest layers are pigment-containing melanocytes that give the skin color and protect the outer cell layers from the damaging effects of ultraviolet radiation. Melanocytes have long, thin finger-like projections, called filipodia, that work their way in between the basal cells. The basal and squamous cell layers are in a constant state of change. Division of a basal cell is followed by a process called keratinization, by which the daughter cells are transformed into prickle cells. Keratin is a tough protein that makes the outer cell layer resistant to abrasion. In the final stage of keratinization, the prickle cell loses its nucleus and the now dead and fully keratinized squame eventually flakes off from the surface. Keratinized squames from the scalp are called dandruff.

The digestive tract is made from different kinds of epithelial cells that are specialized for absorbing nutrients from the food we eat and for secreting large quantities of proteins, lipoproteins, and glycoproteins needed both for digestion and to help control the enormous population of intestinal bacteria. These cells have evolved a shape that reflects the directionality of their activity. That is, they either absorb material from the intestinal tract or secrete material into the lumen of the tract. Consequently, these cells have an elongated shape, with one surface helping to form the lumen of the gut. This surface is the only one involved in absorption or secretion. The absorptive, goblet, and paneth cells of the small intestine are striking examples of epithelium. The *absorptive cells* (also known as brush-border cells) absorb nutrients from the intestine along one surface, covered in microvilli (the brush border), that projects into the lumen of the tract. The cytoplasm of these cells is highly polar, with its large population of mitochondria and extensive rough endoplasmic reticulum (ER) localized near the absorptive surface. The mitochondria contain the enzymatic machinery needed to process the incoming nutrients for the final production of ATP (for more on this process, see chapters 2 and 3). These cells, being specialized for absorption, do not have an extensive Golgi complex. *Goblet cells* are devoted to the secretion of mucus into the gut, which serves to lubricate the walls of the intestine, improving absorption and the movement of the gut contents. The cytoplasm of these cells has an extensive RER and a single large Golgi complex, aimed directly at the brush border, that releases

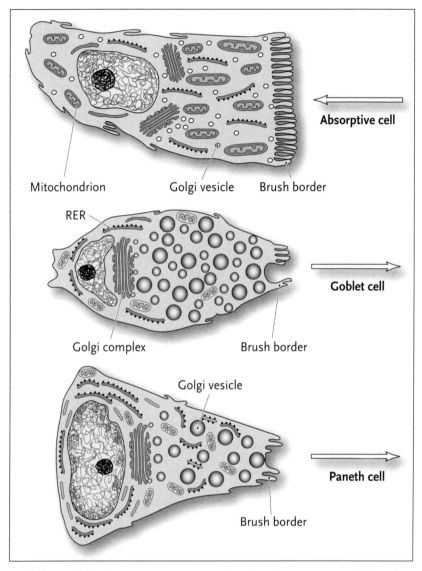

Mitochondrion   Golgi vesicle   Brush border

RER

Absorptive cell

Goblet cell

Golgi complex   Brush border

Golgi vesicle

Paneth cell

Brush border

Epithelium of the digestive tract. Essential molecules are extracted from the food we eat by absorptive cells, equipped with many mitochondria to convert the molecules to ATP. Goblet cells secrete mucus into the intestinal tract for lubrication, and paneth cells secrete an antibacterial protein. All these cells have brush borders to maximize the surface area of the membrane, either for secretion or absorption (indicated by the arrows). Goblet and paneth cells, both specialized for secretion, have a single large Golgi complex aimed directly at the brush border that releases enormous vesicles.

enormous vesicles full of mucus (a special kind of glycoprotein). *Paneth cells* are part of the innate immune system (discussed later in this chapter) that helps control bacterial populations in the lumen of the gut

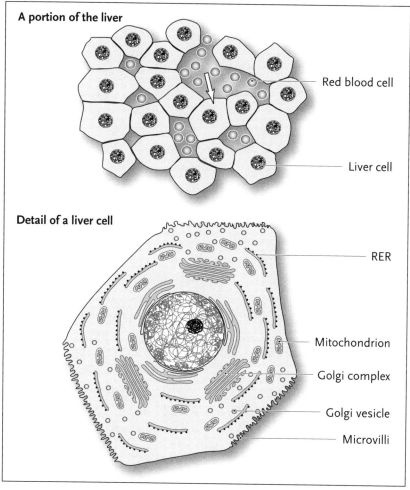

A portion of the liver

Red blood cell

Liver cell

Detail of a liver cell

RER

Mitochondrion

Golgi complex

Golgi vesicle

Microvilli

Organization of the liver and structure of liver cells. The five- or six-sided cells, shown at the top, are loosely arranged around an intricate system of blood vessels and a system of liver canals, called the portal system, that contain bile secretions. A typical liver cell (bottom) has an extensive RER, a large number of mitochondria, and multiple Golgi complexes, in addition to a large polyploid nucleus. The cell membranes lining blood vessels, or the portal system, have many microvilli to facilitate transport into and out of the cell. The magnified cell is from the image at the top. Its position is marked with an arrow.

by secreting proteins called cryptdins that kill bacteria. Like the goblet cells, paneth cells have a highly developed rough ER and Golgi complex. Release of the enormous secretory vesicles is polarized, thus directing all vesicles to the secretory surface.

The liver, weighing almost three pounds, is the heaviest gland in the body and is constructed primarily of epithelium (the liver cells). The five- or six-sided cells are loosely arranged around an intricate system of blood vessels and liver canals. The canals, called the portal system, deliver a substance called bile to the intestinal tract for the digestion of fatty compounds (see top of the liver cells figure on page 103). Liver cells are extremely active metabolically, being involved in detoxifying the blood as well as manufacturing bile. Consequently, these cells have a large number of mitochondria, a very extensive endoplasmic reticulum, and several Golgi complexes. The cell membranes lining blood vessels, or the portal system, have many microvilli to facilitate transport into and out of the cell (see bottom of the liver cells figure on page 103).

To maximize their biosynthetic capabilities, liver cells in humans and many other vertebrates have polyploid nuclei. That is, the DNA content has been duplicated fourfold to eightfold, as compared to a haploid nucleus (i.e., a sperm or an egg nucleus). Consequently, liver cells may be found that are diploid, tetraploid, or octoploid (abbreviated as 2n, 4n, and 8n). Duplicating the genome provides additional copies of crucial genes, all of which may be transcribed simultaneously in order to increase the amount of protein being produced over a given period of time. This is a very clever strategy in that a single octoploid cell is the functional equivalent of four diploid cells. Thus a liver consisting of octoploid cells can be smaller than a diploid liver and still achieve the same output. The practice of maximizing cellular output by duplicating the entire genome is ancient, and this strategy is commonly employed by insects. Insect cells have been found containing a quantity of DNA that is 100,000 times greater than is present in the animal's sperm or eggs.

MUSCLE

As one of the four primary tissues, muscle gives rise to only three cell types: skeletal, cardiac, and smooth muscle. Cardiac muscle forms the

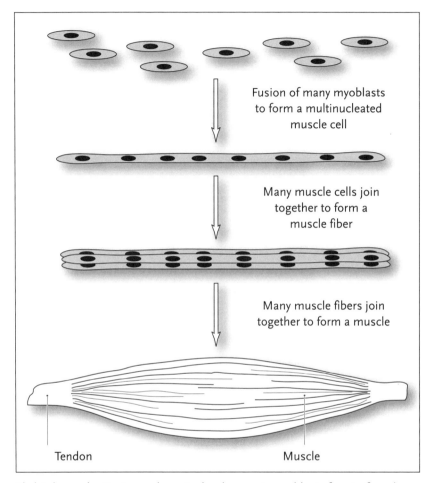

Fusion of many myoblasts to form a multinucleated muscle cell

Many muscle cells join together to form a muscle fiber

Many muscle fibers join together to form a muscle

Tendon   Muscle

Skeletal muscle. During embryonic development, myoblasts fuse to form long, multinucleated muscle cells. The filamentous muscle cells, also called myofibrils, bundle together to form muscle fibers. Finally, many muscle fibers are joined together to form a muscle, anchored at both ends by tendons.

heart; smooth muscle is found in the digestive tract, blood vessels, and the uterine lining; and skeletal muscles move the limbs, tongue, and eyes.

Skeletal muscle is formed during embryonic development, when myoblasts fuse to form a multinucleated muscle cell (also known as a myofibril). Dozens of muscle cells join together to form a muscle fiber, after which the fibers are joined together to make a muscle. The con-

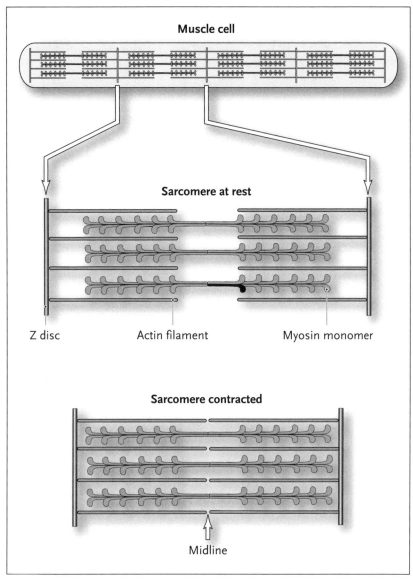

Muscle cell

Sarcomere at rest

Z disc   Actin filament   Myosin monomer

Sarcomere contracted

Midline

The sarcomere. A skeletal muscle cell (top) contains many repeats of the basic contraction unit, called a sarcomere. Each sarcomere (middle) is constructed from actin filaments, which are attached to a Z disc, and myosin monomers, the shape of a golf club (black). The Z discs are constructed from the proteins capZ and alpha-actinin. The sarcomere contracts (bottom) when the club, or headend, of the myosin monomers binds to the actin and pulls the Z discs toward the midline (arrow).

tractile unit of a muscle cell is called a sarcomere. These units are kept perfectly aligned during the formation of the muscle fiber and, finally, the muscle itself. In this way, the muscle, composed of thousands of individual sarcomeres all aligned in register, contracts as though it were a single unit. Sarcomeres are constructed from four kinds of protein: actin, myosin, CapZ, and alpha-actinin. Additional, accessory proteins are present, which stabilize muscle structure and help activate contraction. The precise and regularly repeating arrangement of the sarcomeres is visible in microscopic images of skeletal muscle as cross-striations. The sarcomere contracts when the myosin heads bind to the actin and pull the Z discs toward the center of the sarcomere, which is called the midline. This description of muscle contraction, called the sliding-filament model (so named because the actin "filament" slides along the myosin), was first proposed almost 50 years ago by the British physiologist Sir Andrew Huxley (half brother of Aldous Huxley, the author of *Brave New World*). Huxley based his model on the biochemical analysis of contracting muscles, as well as microscopic images of relaxed and contracting skeletal muscle.

Muscle, like neurons, is an excitable tissue, meaning that it responds to electrochemical signals. Neurons pass the signal along to other neurons in a complex communication network, whereas muscles use the signal to activate contraction. When we move an arm, a leg, or a finger, it is because our brain sends a signal to a neuromuscular junction; a place where the nerve fiber contacts the muscle. The neural stimulus initiates the release of calcium from an internal storage depot, which activates simultaneous contraction of every sarcomere in the muscle. The length of time the calcium remains free depends on the length of the stimulus. If we pick up a heavy object and hold it in the air for a while, the muscle receives a steady stream of neural stimulation, thus keeping the muscle's concentration of free calcium at high levels. When we set the object down, the neural stimulation stops, and the calcium is immediately returned to its storage depot so the muscle can relax.

Cardiac muscle has the same sarcomere-based contraction machinery as that found in skeletal muscle, and thus is another example of striated muscle. The main difference between cardiac muscle and skeletal muscle is that the cardiac muscle has large numbers of

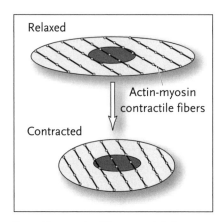

Relaxed

Actin-myosin contractile fibers

Contracted

Smooth muscle. Fibers containing actin and myosin span the cell diagonally with respect to the long axis. Contraction of these fibers pulls the ends of the cell toward the center, greatly reducing its overall length.

gap junctions between the muscle cells, permitting a neural signal to pass freely through every cell in the organ. Consequently, a single impulse will stimulate all the cells simultaneously, allowing the heart to beat as a single unit.

Smooth muscle gets its name from the fact that the contraction machinery is not organized into a sarcomere, and therefore these muscles have a smooth, rather than striated, appearance. Contraction is based on a simple and probably ancient arrangement of actin-myosin filaments. These filaments are arranged in a diagonal pattern from one end of the cell to the other, and as they contract, they pull the ends of the cell toward the center, greatly reducing its overall length. Smooth muscle is not capable of the speed or force of contraction that is typical for striated muscles, but they are ideal for tissues that require slow, rhythmic contractions, such as intestine or uterine lining.

Cells of the Immune System

The human immune system is composed of a diverse group of white blood cells that are divided into three major categories, all of which are derived from connective tissue: granulocytes, monocytes, and lymphocytes (see figure page 109). Granulocytes have a distinctive, lobular nucleus and are phagocytic (can eat cells and viruses). Monocytes are large phagocytic cells with an irregularly shaped nucleus. The largest monocytes, the macrophages, can engulf whole bacteria as well as damaged and senescent body cells. Lymphocytes have a smooth morphology and a large round nucleus. T-lymphocytes (also called T cells) and natural killer (NK) cells deal primarily with coordinating the immune response and with killing already infected body cells. B-lymphocytes (B cells) are nonphagocytic; they deal with an invading microbe by releasing antibodies.

Phagocytosis of an invading microbe by granulocytes and monocytes represents a first-line defense called the innate response. All animals are capable of mounting this kind of defense. Activation of the

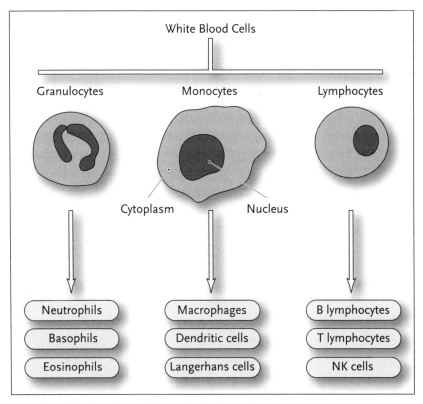

White blood cells. These cells are divided into three major categories: granulocytes, monocytes, and lymphocytes. Granulocytes have a distinctive, lobular nucleus and are phagocytic (eat cells, viruses, and debri). Monocytes are large cells with an irregularly shaped nucleus. All monocytes are phagocytic; the largest members, the macrophages, can engulf whole bacteria and damaged or senescent body cells. Lymphocytes have a smooth morphology with a large round nucleus. B-lymphocytes are nonphagocytic but produce antibodies. T-lymphocytes and natural killer (NK) cells coordinate the immune response and can force infected cells to commit suicide.

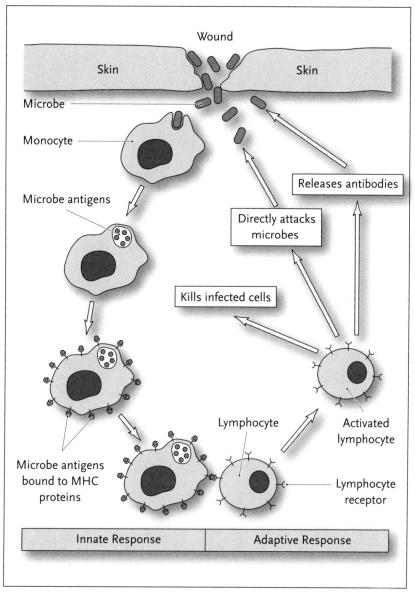

Innate and adaptive immune response. Phagocytosis of invading microbes is called the innate response. In higher vertebrates, microbe antigens, bound to special monocyte surface proteins called the major histocompatibility complex (MHC), are then presented to lymphocytes. Contact between the lymphocyte receptor and the antigen activates the lymphocyte and the adaptive response, consisting of a three-prong attack on the microbe and microbe-infected cells.

lymphocytes leads to a more powerful, second line of defense called the adaptive response, which is found only in higher vertebrates. The adaptive response is initiated by monocytes, specifically, dendritic and Langerhans cells. These cells, after engulfing a virus or bacteria, literally tear the microbe apart and then embed the pieces, now called antigens, in their membrane. The antigens are presented to lymphocytes, which become activated when their receptors bind to the microbial antigens. Activated B-lymphocytes secrete antibodies specifically designed for that particular microbe. Activated T-lymphocytes and NK cells attack the microbe directly but are primarily concerned with locating and killing infected body cells.

The adaptive system can remember a pathogen long after it has been removed from the body. This is why a specific bacteria or virus cannot make us sick twice. Once infected, we develop a natural, lifelong immunity. We can also immunize ourselves against many diseases by injecting a crippled version of the pathogen or specific antigens from a pathogen into our bloodstream. This concoction of bits and pieces from a pathogen, called an immunizing serum, activates the adaptive response, leading to a lasting (though not always lifelong) immunity against the disease.

·7·

NEURONS

Pushing Back the Night

A world without neurons is a dark world, populated by cells, plants, and simple creatures that never see the light of day. That world is a place devoid of vision, where there are no fish in the sea and no animals on the land; where there is no music, no laughter, no emotion, and no intellect. The first cells appeared on Earth 3.5 billion years ago, but life as we know it really began with the appearance of the neuron, about 2 billion years ago.

Neurons, and the things they do, defy the imagination. They make it possible for us to instantly recognize friends that walk into a room. We can tell at a glance if they are happy or sad, and whether they are wearing the same clothes they wore the day before. We can talk to them, for hours on end sometimes, or we can get up and dance around the room. Neurons make all this possible. They do it by forming intricate communication networks, usually consisting of billions of cells. By sending signals, fast and furious, through that network, neurons let us see the world, shape our intellect, and give us our personality.

We have only a vague notion of how neural networks accomplish so much. If we dwell on our personality and the thing psychiatrists call a persona, or self-image, it is difficult to see how these intangible, possibly spiritual, aspects of our brain are generated by neurons simply talking to one another. Equally difficult to understand is the manner by which these networks store and access memories. We know exactly how much memory our personal computers have; it is advertised with every machine. Yet the memory capacity of our own brain is still a mystery. Research in this area is still highly speculative, but many scientists believe the memory capacity of the human brain is infinite. This estimate is based on the observation that on any given day, we always have room for new memories. We never seem to reach that point in time when we have to stop and say, "Sorry, teacher, I can't learn any more, my brain is full." Skeptics would argue that our brains simply erase old memories to make room for the new. We do this sort of thing all the time with our computers. And yet, psychologists insist that under hypnosis, people are able to remember things they once thought were lost. The memories are there, but sometimes we have trouble retrieving them.

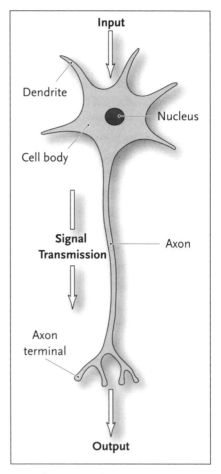

Neural anatomy. A neuron receives signals at finger-like projections from the cell body, called dendrites, and passes them on to other neurons through an elongated process called an axon. The tip of an axon, which often branches into several terminals, makes contact with the dendrites of other neurons.

Neural Anatomy

Neurons are cells that are specially designed for communication and, like computers or other communication hardware, have a polarized anatomy that contains structures for receiving input, and other structures for processing the output. A signal, in the form of an electrochemical current, enters a neuron at finger-like projections, called dendrites, and is passed along

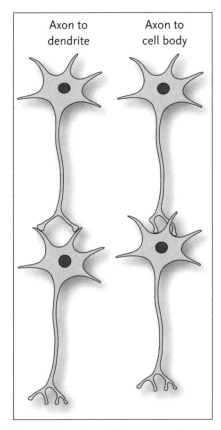

Axon to dendrite

Axon to cell body

Synaptic junctions. The synapse is usually formed between the axon, and one or more dendrites, but axons may also form a synapse with the cell body.

to another neuron through the axon, a single projection, much longer than a dendrite. Signal reception, propagation through the cell, and transmission to another neuron takes less than a millisecond and travels at a rate of 120 meters/sec (270 miles/hr). Every axon forms a communication junction, called a synapse, with a dendrite or the cell body (soma) of another neuron. This simple scheme, repeated millions of times, makes possible the immensely complex neural circuitry of an animal's brain.

Signal Transduction

Propagation of a signal from one neuron to another depends on the coordinated operation of ion channels, located in the cell's membrane. Ion channels vary according to the type of ion that can pass through them, most commonly sodium (Na^+) and calcium (Ca^{++}), and the mechanism by which they are activated. Ligand-gated (Lg) ion channels are activated, or opened, when a signaling molecule, called a ligand, binds to the channel. Lg Na^+ channels are the most common type and serve to initiate neural signaling. Voltage-gated (Vg) channels are opened by an electrical stimulus. The most common channels of this kind permit the entry of Na^+ or Ca^{++} ions.

When Na^+ channels are closed, the ion concentration is greater on the exterior surface of the neuronal membrane than it is on the inside of the cell. Thus the exterior is positively charged relative to the interior.

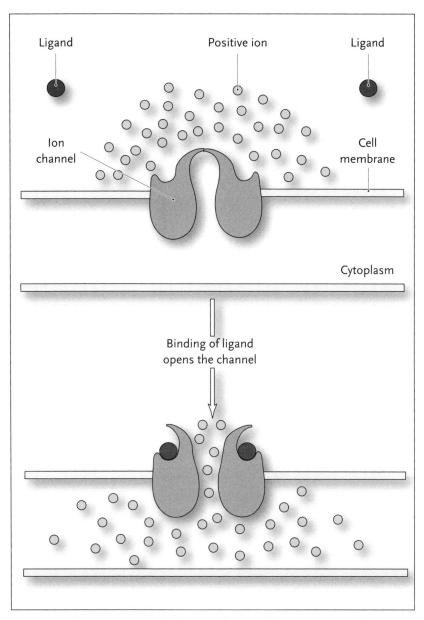

Ligand-gated (Lg) ion channel. The closed channel keeps positively charged ions outside the cell, and in this state, the membrane is said to be polarized (i.e., positive on the outside, relative to the inside). The channel opens when bound to a signaling (ligand) molecule, allowing the ions to rush inside, thus de-polarizing the membrane and initiating an electric current.

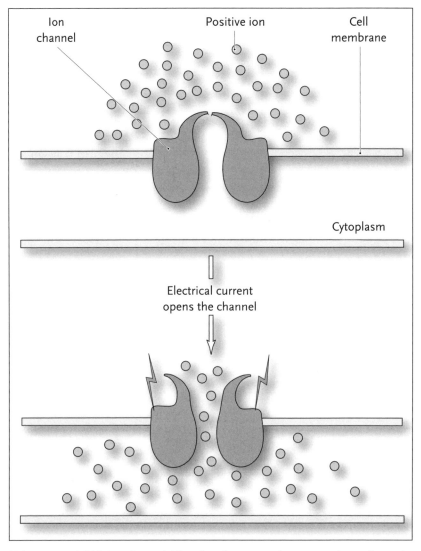

Voltage-gated (Vg) ion channel. The electric current that opens these channels originates with the opening of ligand-gated channels, after which Vg channels are opened by the current generated by other Vg channels.

In this resting state, the membrane is said to be polarized, and the potential difference across the membrane, known as the voltage, is relatively high. When Lg ion channels open, the Na^+ rushes inside the cell, and in so doing, establishes an electrical current. The same applies to a Vg Na$^+$ channel or a Vg Ca^{++} channel.

Neurons receive, propagate, and transmit signals by coordinating the activation of Lg Na$^+$ channels, Vg Na$^+$ channels, and finally Vg Ca^{++} channels. Lg Na$^+$ channels are always located in dendritic membranes (the input end of the cell). A special ligand, known as a neurotransmitter, sent by a neuron, binds to and activates Lg Na$^+$ channels. The opening of these channels initiates an electrical stimulus through membrane depolarization. This signal spreads electrotonically, or passively, through the cytoplasm, and decays rapidly with distance, but usually has enough strength to activate the first Vg Na$^+$ channels, located in the axonal membrane close to the cell body. The signal propagates along the axon, toward the axonal terminus, by sequential activation of Vg Na$^+$ channels. The strength of this signal is boosted each time a Vg channel opens, so it does not decay over the full length of the axon. The signal through the axon is called a spike potential, because the opening of each channel results in a renewed burst (spike) of the electrical current. Finally, the Vg Na$^+$ channels activate Vg Ca^{++}

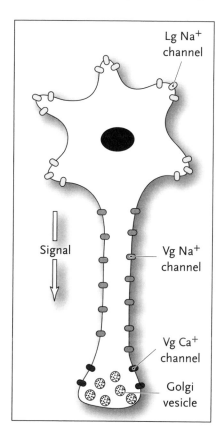

Signal transmission. A ligand (neurotransmitter) binds to the Lg sodium (Na$^+$) channels, depolarizing the membrane and initiating an electric current that opens the first Vg Na$^+$ channels in the axon. The signal propagates along the axon by sequential activation of the Vg Na$^+$ channels. Finally, the axonal current activates the Vg calcium (Ca^{++}) channels. Influx of calcium stimulates exocytosis of the Golgi vesicles, containing neurotransmitters that send the signal on to another neuron.

channels, located at the axonal terminus. The influx of calcium stimulates exocytosis of Golgi vesicles (fusion of the vesicles with the cell membrane), containing neurotransmitters that send the signal on to other neurons.

Signal propagation along the axon is unidirectional because the Na^+ channels, just behind the advancing signal, are deactivated. Special Na^+ pumps, driven by the hydrolysis of ATP, return the ion to the extra cellular space, thus repolarizing the membrane. This also serves to reactivate the channels, in preparation for the next signal. The Vg Na^+ channels are capable of processing 500 signals per second, and depolarization of the membrane involves the passage of up to 10 million Na^+ per second.

The Synaptic Junction

The connection between an axon and a dendrite is called a synapse. Although neurons communicate through the synapse, they do not actually touch one another. Close inspection of a synapse shows a small gap separating the axon from the dendrite. A signal is transmitted across the gap by the release of neurotransmitters that are stored at the axon terminus in Golgi-derived vesicles. The vesicles travel to the axon terminus on a railroad-like transport network constructed of microtubules. When a neuron receives a signal, the Golgi vesicles, at the terminus, are released from the microtubules and fuse with the axonal membrane, dumping their cargo into the synaptic gap. The neurotransmitters quickly diffuse across the gap and bind to receptors on the dendritic membrane, triggering an electrochemical impulse in the target neuron, thus completing transmission of the signal. This may seem like an awkward way for neurons to signal each other, but the synaptic gap, and the use of neurotransmitters, is crucial for maintaining the strength of the signal over a network that consists of 100 billion cells. Each neuron in such a circuit boosts the signal to its original strength, in a manner analogous to the signal boost that each Vg Na^+ channel provides as the signal travels along each axon.

Myelination

A neural circuit, much like an ordinary household electrical circuit, works better if the axons are insulated. Electrical wire is insulated with a plastic

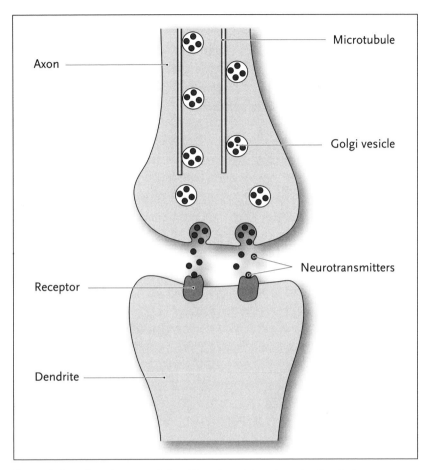

Synaptic junction. Axons and dendrites do not touch each other but are separated by a small gap called the synapse or synaptic junction. A signal is transmitted by the release of small molecules called neurotransmitters that are stored at the axon terminus in Golgi vesicles. Binding of the neurotransmitter to the receptor on the dendrite membrane completes the transmission. The Golgi vesicles travel to the axon terminus on a transportation network constructed from microtubules.

coating, but neurons are insulated by special cells that form a coating, called myelin, around each axon. Myelin is constructed from cells called oligodendrocytes and Schwann cells that wrap around axons to form a protective multilayered sheath. Oligodendrocytes, located in the central nervous system (CNS, consisting of the brain and spinal cord), can myeli-

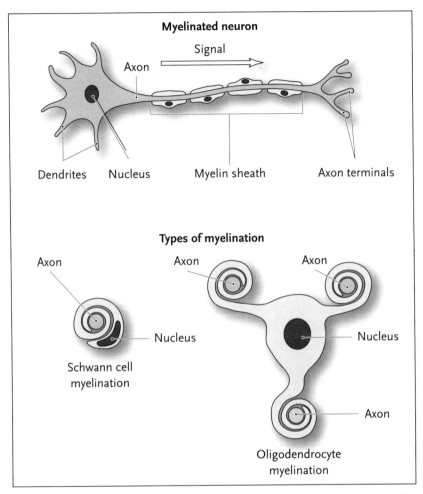

Neural signaling and myelination. Communication between neurons is much more efficient when the axons are insulated with a myelin sheath. Myelin is made by Schwann cells or oligodendrocytes wrapping around the axon. Oligodendrocytes can insulate more than one axon at a time.

nate more than one axon at a time. Schwann cells, located in the peripheral nervous system (i.e., any nerves outside the CNS, such as those in the toes and fingers), wrap around a single axon. The existence of the myelin sheath greatly complicates medical procedures aimed at repairing a severed spinal cord or neural damage caused by Alzheimer's or Parkinson's disease.

Neurotransmitters

Neurons synthesize the ligand, called a neurotransmitter, that is released at the axonal terminus to relay a signal to another neuron. Neurotransmitters are divided into two major groups. The first group is composed of fast, direct neurotransmitters that include acetylcholine (synthesized from acetyl-CoA and choline) and several amino acids (glutamate, aspartate, gamma-amino butyric acid, and glycine). The second group is composed of slow, indirect neurotransmitters that include the monoamines (derived from various amino acids), such as epinephrine, dopamine, and serotonin. This group also includes a large number of neuropeptides. Fast, direct neurotransmitters bind to receptors that are ion channels. By contrast, the slow, indirect neurotransmitters bind to receptors that are linked to a signaling pathway and thus modulate the behavior of the target neuron through a series of biochemical steps, rather than generating an electrical current.

Acetylcholine (ACh) is one of the most ubiquitous neurotransmitters, being used by most vertebrate species in motor neurons (neurons that directly stimulate muscle) and various neurons in the CNS. Neurons that use ACh are referred to as being cholinergic. GABA and glycine are both inhibitory neurotransmitters released by neurons in the CNS and peripheral nervous system (PNS) in vertebrates, crustaceans, and worms. Glutamine is an excitatory neurotransmitter found in the CNS of vertebrates, insects, and crustaceans. Glutamate receptors participate in modifying synaptic behavior and organization during long-term potentiation (learning and memory).

Norepinephrine (NE), synthesized from the amino acid phenylalanine, is released by various neurons in the CNS, as well as cells in the adrenal gland. Neurons releasing NE are said to be adrenergic. Psychoactive drugs, such as mescaline (from the peyote cactus), interfere with NE signal transmission in the CNS. Amphetamines mimic the function of NE, and cocaine interferes with NE inactivation, thus prolonging the stimulation of an adrenergic network. Dopamine, synthesized from the amino acid tyrosine, occurs throughout the CNS and acts through a signaling pathway. Dopamine is primarily a neuromodulator and is able to dampen the excitability of the target neuron. Parkinson's disease is a neurological disorder characterized by the degeneration and death of dopaminergic neurons in an area of the brain known as the substantia nigra. Serotonin, synthesized from the amino acid tryptophan, also occurs throughout the CNS. Some of the receptors are ion channels, while others are linked to signaling pathways.

Neuropeptides, consisting of about 30 amino acids, are widely distributed throughout the CNS and, like serotonin, bind to receptors that are ion channels or are linked to signaling pathways. One group of neuropeptides, called the endogenous opioids, are involved in regulating neural circuits controlling many physiological processes, including behavior, appetite, pain tolerance, stress, and shock. They are also involved in regulating the neuroendocrine system, primarily through their ability to reduce the excitability of neurons and neuroendocrine cells.

Neural Circuits

Neural circuits probably began with a single neuron acting as both a receptor cell and as a motor neuron capable of stimulating muscle or other tissue. This simple scheme evolved into a more elaborate system with the addition of specialized neurons, situated between the receptor and the target tissue. The additional circuitry became the central nervous system, capable of processing and evaluating the original stimulus before any action is taken.

Neural circuits in the human brain are enormously complex, consisting of more than 10 billion neurons, each forming thousands of synaptic junctions with other neurons. In total, it has been estimated that the human brain has more than a trillion synaptic junctions. One type of neuron in the cerebellum, called the Purkinje cell, has thousands of dendrites, receiving inputs from more than 200,000 other neurons. Circuits involving these neurons are part of the brain's machinery for controlling complex movements.

The complexity of the brain circuitry increases in humans, and other mammals, soon after birth. The increased complexity is not due to an increase in the number of neurons but rather is due to an increase in the number of synaptic junctions. The addition of new synapses increases the integrative and analytic capabilities of the circuit and may be necessary for the storage of new memories. Experiments with rats

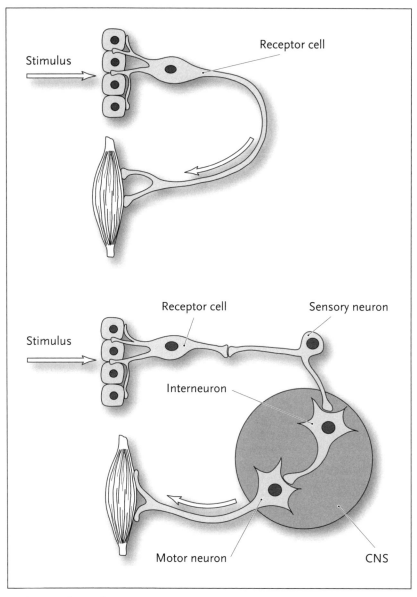

Evolution of neural circuits. Circuits evolved from single-cell circuits consisting of a neuron that had the duel function of a receptor cell and a motor neuron capable of stimulating a muscle or other tissue. More advanced circuits includes sensory neurons and a central nervous system (CNS), consisting of many different kinds of neurons that process and evaluate the stimulus before activating a motor neuron or other output neurons.

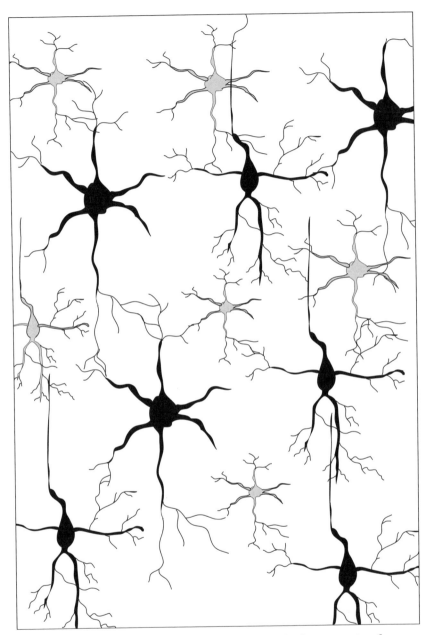

A neural circuit in the mammalian brain. Circuits in the brain consist of billions of neurons, each forming thousands of synaptic junctions with other neurons. These complex, highly integrated circuits give us our intellect, our emotions, our ability to see the world, and much more.

have shown that animals reared in a boring environment, with minimal visual stimulation, have fewer synapses than rats reared in stimulating environments or subjected to long-term training exercises. Extensive training and learning exercises also modify pre-existing synapses in several ways: synaptic contacts increase in size, the number of Golgi vesicles stored at the axonal terminus increases, and there is an increase in the number of Ca^{++} channels in the pre-synaptic membrane. All these changes are part of a complex process, known as long-term potentiation, that remodels the circuitry for enhanced functionality and memory storage.

Summary

If neurons had never appeared on our planet, there would still be luxurious plant communities covering the surface of the earth, microbes would be everywhere, and the seas would contain simple creatures, like coral and sponges. All these organisms are constructed from cells that communicate with each other, but they do so through a slow process involving the exchange of molecules that bind to cell-surface receptors. Neurons, by exploiting the properties of ion channels, introduced a lightning-fast form of communication, without which the progression from single cells to complex multicellular bodies would not have been possible.

.8.

RESOURCE CENTER

Studying the cell requires a great deal of hardware, technology, and experimental procedures. This chapter provides additional information that covers light microscopy, histology and histochemistry, and recombinant DNA technology.

Light Microscopy

Microscopes are among the oldest of scientific instruments, and yet they are just as important today as they were 120 years ago when microbiologists used them to study bacteria and the many diseases they cause. The earliest microscopes, invented in the 1600s by Antonie van Leeuwenhoek were single lenses mounted in a brass frame that were held in the hand or attached to a table. These simple magnifying glasses could resolve bacteria and other microbes but were extremely difficult, and tiring, to use.

By the 1700s, compound microscopes, using two or more lenses, were being made that offered higher magnifications than Leeuwenhoek's microscope and were much easier to use, but the image quality was not as good. These microscopes consisted essentially of an eyepiece, a metal tube, and an objective that formed the initial magnified image of the object. Adding two or more lenses together increased the overall power of a microscope but, at the same time, introduced optical artifacts that seriously degraded the image. The two most important of these artifacts are spherical and chromatic aberration.

Spherical and chromatic aberrations arise as a natural consequence of the way light behaves when it passes through a glass lens, which has a higher density than the air around it. There are two simple rules of geometric optics that govern this behavior. First, light travels in a straight path, and second, the path bends (refracts) at an interface between two transparent media (i.e., the air and the lens). Lenses are designed with curved surfaces to magnify an object, and to bring the image of that object to a single focal point. Spherical aberration occurs when light rays from an object are refracted by different parts of the lens and, therefore, do not come to a single focal point, producing an image that is fuzzy and out of focus. Chromatic aberration is a consequence of the multiwavelength composition of white light, ranging from red (long wavelength) to blue (short wavelength). The extent to which light is refracted at an interphase

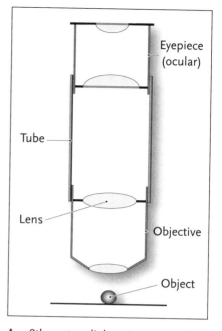

An 18th-century light microscope. The image is magnified by the objective and brought to focus at the eye by the eyepiece. The eyepiece and objective are compound-lens systems that give high magnification but poor resolution and image quality.

depends on its wavelength, being high for blue light and low for red light. Therefore, the blue and red components of white light are refracted by a lens to separate focal points, producing a fuzzy image that has a red and blue halo.

In 1868, the German physicist, Ernst Abbe, discovered a way to construct objectives containing lens pairs and triplets that corrected chromatic and spherical aberration simultaneously. These lens systems, called apochromatic objectives, provide clear and undistorted images at the highest magnification possible (1,000x) while retaining a high resolution. The measure for resolution is the smallest distance at which two points can still be discerned. A resolution of one micrometer

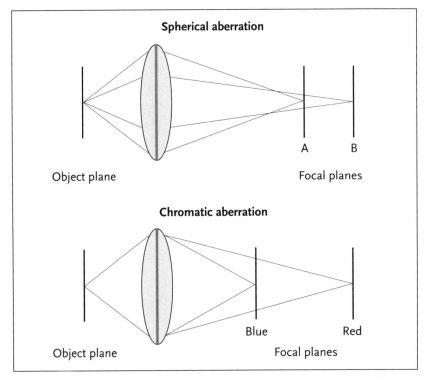

Spherical aberration

Object plane

A B

Focal planes

Chromatic aberration

Object plane

Blue

Red

Focal planes

Spherical and chromatic lens aberrations. Spherical aberration is caused by variations in the amount of refraction that occurs over the surface of the lens. Consequently, light passing through peripheral areas of the lens come to a different focal point (A) than light passing through central regions (B). Chromatic aberration occurs because the amount of refraction is greater for blue light than it is for red light. Thus these two wavelengths, and all wavelengths in between, come to different focal points.

(μm), for instance, indicates that two objects one μm apart can still be seen as separate objects, whereas if the objects were 0.5 μm apart, they would appear to be a single object. Apochromatic objectives provide a resolution of 0.4 μm, very close to the theoretical limit for light microscopes of 0.2 μm (a distance of 0.2 μm is about 1/500th the diameter of a period on this page). The high resolution, and clarity of the image, provided by apochromatic objectives made it possible for scientists to study the structure and function of individual cells in a way that was never before possible. The quality of Abbe's lenses has never been surpassed, and apochromatic objectives are still standard on light microscopes today.

With the lens system perfected, microscopes quickly evolved from a simple monocular construction to binocular compound microscopes that are equipped with rotating turrets, holding a variety of objectives, camera attachments, video equipment, and special filtering systems for observing fluorescent images. In addition, microscopes with special optical systems, known as phase contrast and Nomarski's interference, were invented in the 1950s that made possible the observation of living cells without having to stain them with dyes. An important advance in the field of microscopy came with the introduction of the fluorescent microscope, an instrument that is used to observe cells and tissue sections that have been stained with fluorescent dyes. This microscope has standard objectives, but it includes special optical filters, and a beam splitter, for observing cells and tissues emitting fluorescent light. A fluorescent dye is a molecule that absorbs light of one wavelength, emitting it at another, longer wavelength.

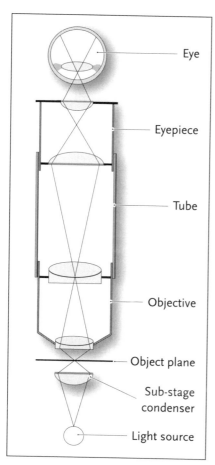

Eye

Eyepiece

Tube

Objective

Object plane

Sub-stage condenser

Light source

A light microscope corrected for chromatic and spherical aberration. Light is focused on the object by a condenser to enhance image quality and contrast. Chromatic and spherical aberrations are corrected at the objective with precisely ground lens-pairs or triplets (two or three lenses fitted together). High power objectives (100x) may have up to 10 separate lenses to correct for aberrations. The example shown at left is a 10x objective, consisting of four lenses.

A 19th-century monocular microscope. These instruments were capable of high resolution but were difficult to use for extended periods of time. *(Courtesy of Dr. Joseph Panno)*

An example is the molecule fluorescein, which emits green light, at 520 nanometers (nm), when stimulated with blue light at 450 nm.

Monocular microscopes used at the turn of the 20th century could be carried around in a container not much bigger than a shoebox. Modern, fully equipped research microscopes are not only more powerful, they are also much bigger, weighing more than 100 pounds, and easily filling the top of a lab bench. Indeed, some of these microscopes are so large, and so elaborate, they often need their own room.

Histology and Histochemistry

Histology and histochemistry represent an overlapping collection of techniques that are used to study the structure and chemical properties of intact tissues. Histology means literally the study of tissue, whereas, histochemistry refers to the use of specific stains to enhance the detection of microscopic detail, based on known chemical or physical properties of the tissue. Thus progress in histochemistry improved histology.

The microscopic characterization of human tissues, organs, and more than 200 human cell types, some of which are described in chapters 6 and 7, were originally obtained with a combination of histological and histochemical techniques. Studies involving these procedures are generally conducted on tissue sections or tissue smears that have been

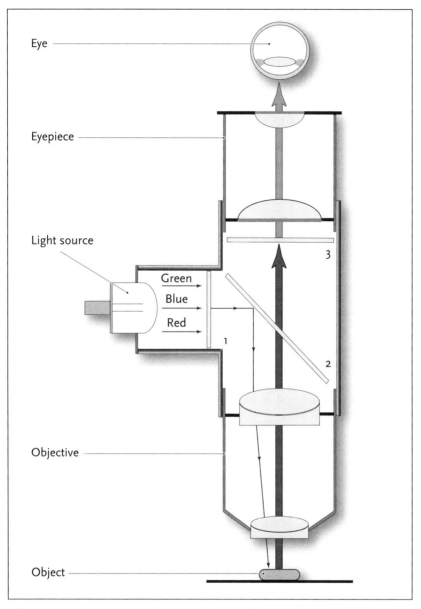

A fluorescence microscope. A light source is filtered by a barrier filter (1) that blocks passage of all wavelengths, except for blue light, which is deflected by a beam-splitting mirror (2), directing it through the objective, where it stimulates fluorescent molecules in the object. Fluorescent light from the object passes freely through the beam splitter and is filtered of spurious fluorescence by a second barrier filter (3) before reaching the eye.

preserved with a chemical fixative and then stained with colored dyes. Histological preparations of tissue sections form the basis for our understanding of organ structure at the cellular level and is indispensable for the study of physiology. Histochemical analysis is usually focused more at the cellular level and was crucial for localizing DNA to the cell nucleus and for tracking the movement of molecules between the various subcellular compartments. Prominent examples included the movement of RNA from the nucleus to the cytoplasm, the movement of certain proteins from the cytoplasm back to the nucleus, and the transport of other proteins through the endoplasmic reticulum and Golgi complex.

HISTOLOGY

Tissues are usually fixed, or preserved, before they are stained with a dye. Two fixatives that are commonly used are formalin (10 percent formaldehyde solution) and a mixture of alcohol and glacial acetic acid (3:1), called Clark's solution. Formalin is preferred for most applica-

A modern binocular microscope that is used in cancer research. This particular instrument is connected to a computer, which displays the image field on the monitor and is equipped with software for analyzing and enhancing the image. *(Courtesy of Jean-Paul Chassenet/Photo Researchers, Inc.)*

tions, but Clark's solution is ideal for blood or chromosome smears. Staining tissues with various dyes to enhance the contrast of their microscopic image is a standard histological procedure. This approach takes advantage of biochemical differences between the various cellular compartments. The nucleus, for example, consists primarily of the negatively charged DNA, whereas the cytoplasm carries a net positive charge. Thus a positively charged dye, such as hemotoxylin, can be used to stain the nucleus, while a negatively charged dye, such as eosin, will stain the cytoplasm. These two dyes are normally used together; hemotoxylin stains the nucleus blue, while eosin counterstains the cytoplasm pink.

HISTOCHEMISTRY

Fixed tissues can be stained for specific cellular compounds such as DNA, RNA, lipids, and specific proteins. Of these procedures, the most important is the Feulgen reaction, which is used for detecting DNA. The Feulgen reaction involves hydrolyzing DNA nucleotides in a strong acid solution to expose aldehyde groups. The aldehydes, in turn, react with a special dye solution, called Schiff's reagent, resulting in a deep purple color. The Feulgen reaction is specific for DNA and does not stain other molecules in the nucleus, or the cytoplasm. This method has been used to determine the amount of DNA in individual cell nuclei and to assess the degree of chromatin condensation.

Recombinant DNA Technology

Recombinant technology is a collection of procedures that make it possible to isolate a gene and produce enough of it for a detailed study of its structure and function. Central to this technology is the ability to construct libraries of DNA fragments that represent the genetic repertoire of an entire organism, or of a specific cell type. Constructing these libraries involves splicing different pieces of DNA together to form a novel or recombinant genetic entity, from which the procedure derives its name. DNA cloning and library construction were made possible by the discovery of DNA modifying enzymes that can seal two pieces of DNA together, or can cut DNA at sequence-specific sites. Many of the procedures that are part of recombinant technology, such as DNA sequencing or filter hybridization, were developed in order to characterize DNA fragments that were isolated from cells or gene libraries. Obtaining the sequence of a gene has made it possible to study the organization of the genome, but more important, it has provided a simple way of determining the protein sequence, and the expression profile for any gene.

DNA-MODIFYING ENZYMES

Two of the most important enzymes used in recombinant technology are those that can modify DNA by sealing two fragments together, and others that can cut DNA at specific sites. The first modifying enzyme to be discovered was DNA ligase, an enzyme that can join two pieces of

RESTRICTION ENZYMES

Enzyme	Source	Sequence
EcoRI	Escherichia coli	
HindII	Haemophilus influenzae	
BamHI	Bacillus amyloliquefaciens	
PstI	Providencia situartii	

Arrows indicate the sites at which the enzyme cuts the DNA.

DNA together and is an important component of the cell's DNA replication and repair machinery. Other DNA modifying enzymes, called restriction enzymes, cut DNA at sequence-specific sites, with different members of the family cutting at different sites. Restriction enzymes are isolated from bacteria, and since their discovery in 1970, more than 90 such enzymes have been isolated from more than 230 bacterial strains; a few examples are shown in the figure on page 135.

The name "restriction enzyme" is cryptic and calls for an explanation. During the period when prokaryotes began to appear on earth, their environment contained a wide assortment of molecules that were released into the soil or water by other cells, either deliberately or when the cells died. DNA of varying lengths was among these molecules and was readily taken up by living cells. If the foreign DNA contained complete genes from a competing bacterial species, there was the real possibility that those genes could have been transcribed and translated by the host cell with potentially fatal results. As a precaution, prokaryotes evolved a set of enzymes that would *restrict* the foreign DNA population by cutting it up into smaller pieces before being broken down completely to individual nucleotides.

GEL ELECTROPHORESIS

This procedure is used to separate different DNA and RNA fragments in a slab of agar or polyacrylamide subjected to an electric field. Nucleic acids carry a negative charge and thus will migrate toward a positively charged electrode. The gel acts as a sieving medium that impedes the movement of the molecules. Thus the rate at which the fragments migrate is a function of their size; small fragments migrate more rapidly than large fragments. The gel, containing the samples, is run submerged in a special pH-regulated solution, or buffer, containing a nucleic acid–specific dye, ethidium bromide. This dye produces a strong reddish-yellow fluorescence when exposed to ultraviolet (UV) radiation. Consequently, after electrophoresis, the nucleic acid can be detected by photographing the gel under UV illumination.

DNA CLONING

In 1973, scientists discovered that restriction enzymes, DNA ligase, and bacterial plasmids could be used to clone DNA molecules. Plasmids are

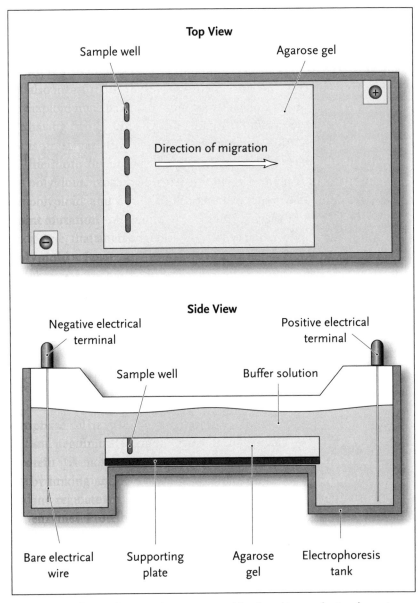

Top View

Sample well

Agarose gel

Direction of migration

Side View

Negative electrical terminal

Positive electrical terminal

Sample well

Buffer solution

Bare electrical wire

Supporting plate

Agarose gel

Electrophoresis tank

Agarose gel electrophoresis. An agarose gel is placed in an electrophoresis tank and submerged in a buffer solution. The electric terminals are connected to a power source, with the sample wells positioned near the negative terminal. When the current is turned on, the negatively charged nucleic acids migrate toward the positive terminal. The migration rate is an inverse function of molecular size (large molecules travel slower than small ones).

small (3–4 kb) circular minichromosomes that occur naturally in bacteria and are often exchanged between cells by passive diffusion. When a bacterium acquires a new plasmid it is said to have been transfected. For bacteria, the main advantage to swapping plasmids is that they often carry antibiotic resistance genes so that a cell sensitive to ampicillin can become resistant simply by acquiring the right plasmid.

The first cloning experiment used a plasmid from *Escherichia coli* that was cut with the restriction enzyme *Eco*RI. The plasmid had a single *Eco*RI site so the restriction enzyme simply opened the circular molecule, rather than cutting it up into many useless pieces, Foreign DNA, cut with the same restriction enzyme, was incubated with the plasmid. Because the plasmid and foreign DNA were both cut with *Eco*RI, the DNA could insert itself into the plasmid to form a hybrid, or recombinant plasmid, after which DNA ligase sealed the two together. The reaction mixture was added to a small volume of *E. coli* so that some of the cells could take up the recombinant plasmid before being transferred to a nutrient broth containing streptomycin. Only those cells carrying the recombinant plasmid, which contained an anti-streptomycin gene, could grow in the presence of this antibiotic. Each time the cells divided, the plasmid DNA was duplicated along with the main chromosome. After the cells had grown overnight, the foreign DNA had been amplified, or cloned, billions of times and was easily isolated for sequencing or expression studies.

GENOMIC AND cDNA LIBRARIES

The basic cloning procedure described above not only provides a way to amplify a specific piece of DNA, but it can also be used to construct gene libraries. In this case, however, the cloning vector is a bacteriophage, called lambda. The lambda genome is double-stranded linear DNA of about 40,000 base pairs, much of which can be replaced by foreign DNA without sacrificing the ability of the virus to infect bacteria. This is the great advantage of lambda over a plasmid. Lambda can accommodate very long pieces of DNA, often long enough to contain an entire gene, whereas a plasmid cannot accommodate foreign DNA that is larger than 2,000 base pairs. Moreover, bacteriophage has the natural ability to infect bacteria, so that the efficiency of transfection is 100x greater than it is for plasmids.

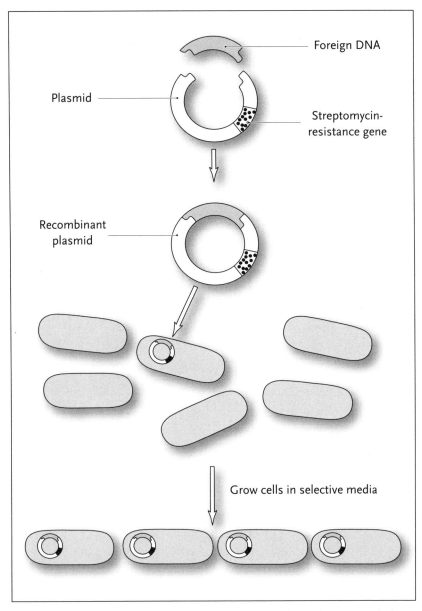

Cloning DNA in a plasmid. The foreign DNA and the plasmid are cut with the same restriction enzyme, allowed to fuse, and then sealed with DNA ligase. The recombinant plasmid is mixed with bacterial cells, some of which pick up the plasmid, allowing them to grow in a culture medium containing streptomycin. The bacteria's main chromosome is not shown.

The construction of a gene library begins by isolating genomic DNA and digesting it with a restriction enzyme to produce fragments of 1,000 to 10,000 base pairs. These fragments are ligated into lambda genomes, which are subjected to a packaging reaction to produce mature viral particles, most of which carry a different piece of the genomic DNA. This collection of viruses is called a genomic library and is used to study the structure and organization of specific genes. Clones from a library such as this contain the coding sequences, in addition to introns, intervening sequences, promoters, and enhancers. An alternative form of a gene library can be constructed by isolating mRNA from a specific cell type. This RNA is converted to the complementary DNA (cDNA) using an RNA-dependent DNA polymerase called reverse transcriptase. The cDNA is ligated to lambda genomes and packaged as for the genomic library. This collection of recombinant viruses is a cDNA library and only contains genes that were being expressed by the cells when the RNA was extracted. It does not include introns or controlling elements because these are lost during transcription and the processing that occurs in the cell to make mature mRNA. Thus a cDNA library is intended for the purpose of studying gene expression and the structure of the coding region only.

LABELING CLONED DNA

Many of the procedures used in the area of recombinant technology were inspired by the events that occur during DNA replication. This includes the labeling of cloned DNA for use as probes in expression studies, DNA sequencing, and PCR (described below). DNA replication involves duplicating one of the strands (the parent, or template strand) by linking nucleotides in an order specified by the template and depends on a large number of enzymes, the most important of which is DNA polymerase. This enzyme, guided by the template strand, constructs a daughter strand by linking nucleotides together. One such nucleotide is deoxyadenine triphosphate (dATP). Deoxyribonucleotides have a single hydroxyl group located at the 3' carbon of the sugar group, while the triphosphate is attached to the 5' carbon. The procedure for labeling DNA probes, developed in 1983, introduces radioactive nucleotides into a DNA molecule. This method supplies DNA polymerase with a single stranded DNA template, a primer, and the four nucleotides, in a buffered solution to induce *in vitro* replication. The daughter strand, which becomes the labeled probe, is made radioactive by including a ^{32}P-labeled nucleotide in the reaction mix. The radioactive nucleotide is usually deoxy-cytosine triphosphate (dCTP), or dATP. The ^{32}P is always part of the α (alpha) phosphate (the phosphate closest to the 5' carbon), as this is the one used by the polymerase to form the phosphodiester bond between nucleotides.

Single-stranded DNA hexamers (six bases long) are used as primers, and these are produced in such a way that they contain all possible permutations of four bases taken six at a time. Randomizing the base sequence for the primers ensures that there will be at least one primer site in a temple that is only 50 bp long. Templates used in labeling reactions such as this are generally 100 to 800 bp long. This strategy of labeling DNA, known as random primer or oligo labeling, is widely used in cloning and in DNA and RNA filter hybridizations (described below).

DNA SEQUENCING

A sequencing reaction developed by the British biochemist Dr. Fred Sanger in 1976 is another technique that takes its inspiration from the natural process of DNA replication. DNA polymerase requires a primer with a free 3' hydroxyl group. The polymerase adds the first nucleotide to this group, and all subsequent bases are added to the 3' hydroxyl of the previous base. Sequencing by the Sanger method is usually

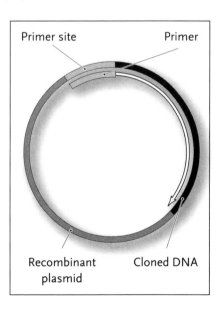

Plasmid primer site for DNA sequencing. The cloned DNA is inserted into the plasmid near an engineered primer site. Once the primer binds to the primer site, the cloned DNA may be replicated, as part of a sequencing reaction, in the direction indicated by the arrow. Only one strand of the double-stranded plasmid and cloned DNA is shown.

performed with the DNA cloned into a plasmid. This simplifies the choice of the initial primers because their sequence can be derived from the known plasmid sequence. An engineered plasmid primer site adjacent to a cloned DNA fragment is shown in the figure on page 140. Once the primer binds to the primer site, the cloned DNA may be replicated. Sanger's innovation involved the synthesis of artificial nucleotides lacking the 3' hydroxyl group, thus producing di-deoxynucleotides (ddATP, ddCTP, ddGTP, and ddTTP). Incorporation of a dideoxynucleotide terminates the growth of the daughter strand at that point, and this can be used to determine the size of each daughter strand. The shortest daughter strand represents the complementary nucleotide at the beginning of the template, whereas the longest strand represents the complementary nucleotide at the end of the template (see table below). The reaction products, consisting of all the daughter strands, are fractionated on a polyacrylamide gel. Polyacrylamide serves

EXAMPLE OF A SEQUENCING REACTION

Tube	Reaction Products	
A	G-C-A-T-C-G-T-C C-G-T-**A**	G-C-A-T-C-G-T-C C-G-T-A-G-C-**A**
T	G-C-A-T-C-G-T-C C-G-**T**	
C	G-C-A-T-C-G-T-C **C**	G-C-A-T-C-G-T-C C-G-T-A-G-**C**
G	G-C-A-T-C-G-T-C C-**G**	G-C-A-T-C-G-T-C C-G-T-A-**G**
	G-C-A-T-C-G-T-C C-G-T-A-G-C-A-**G**	

The Sanger sequencing reaction is set up in four separate tubes, each containing a different dideoxynucleotide (ddATP, ddTTP, ddCTP, and ddGTP). The reaction products are shown for each of the tubes: A (ddATP), T (ddTTP), C (ddCTP), and G (ddGTP). The template strand is GCATCGTC. Replication of the template begins after the primer binds to the primer site on the sequencing plasmid. The dideoxynucleotide terminating the reaction is shown in bold. The daughter strands, all of different lengths, are fractionated on a polyacrylamide gel.

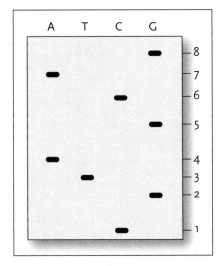

A representation of a sequencing gel. The reaction products (shown in the table on page 141) run from the top to the bottom, with the smallest fragment migrating at the highest rate. The sequence is read beginning with the smallest fragment on the gel (band # 1, in the "C" lane) and ending with the largest fragment at the top (band # 8, in the "G" lane). The sequence is CGTAGCAG. The complementary sequence is GCATCGTC. This is the template strand indicated in the table on page 141.

the same function as agarose. It has the advantage of being a tougher material, essential for the large size of a typical sequencing gel. Some of the nucleotides included in the Sanger reaction are labeled with a radioactive isotope so the fractionated daughter strands can be visualized by drying the gel and then exposing it to X-ray film. Thus the Sanger method uses the natural process of replication to mark the position of each nucleotide in the DNA fragment so the sequence of the cloned DNA can be determined.

The fragments are separated by size using polyacrylamide gel electrophoresis and visualized by exposing the dried gel to X-ray film. A representation of such a gel is shown in the figure at left. The sequence of the daughter strand is read beginning with the smallest fragment at the bottom of the gel and ending with the largest fragment at the top. The sequence of the template strand is obtained simply by taking the complement of the sequence obtained from the gel (the daughter strand).

SOUTHERN AND NORTHERN BLOTTING

One of the most important techniques to be developed, as part of recombinant technology, is the transfer of nucleic acids from an agarose gel to nylon filter paper that can be hybridized to a labeled probe to detect specific genes. This procedure was introduced in 1975 by the Scottish scientist E. M. Southern for transferring DNA and is now known as Southern blotting. Since the DNA is transferred to filter paper, the detection stage is known as filter hybridization. In 1980, the procedure was modified to transfer RNA to nylon membranes for the study of gene expression and, in reference to the original, is called northern blotting.

Northern blotting is used to study the expression of specific genes, and is usually performed on messenger RNA (mRNA). Typical experiments may wish to determine the expression of specific genes in normal, versus cancerous tissue, or tissues obtained from groups of different ages. The RNA is fractionated on an agarose gel and then transferred to a nylon membrane. The paper towels placed on top of the assembly pull the transfer buffer through the gel, eluting the RNA from the gel and trapping it on the membrane. The location of specific mRNA can be determined by hybridizing the membrane to a radiolabeled cDNA or genomic clone. The hybridization procedure involves placing the filter in a buffer solution containing a labeled probe. During a long incubation period, the probe binds to the target sequence immobilized on the membrane. A-T and G-C base pairing mediate the binding between the probe and target.

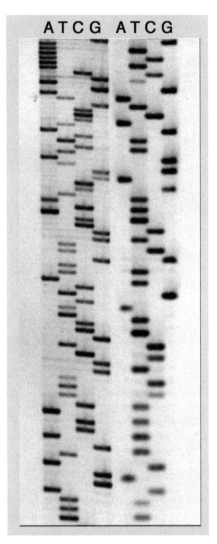

An autoradiogram of a portion of a DNA sequencing gel. A partial sequence (the first 20 bases) of the left set, beginning at the bottom of the "T" lane, is TTTAGGATGACCACTTTGGC. *(Courtesy of Dr. Joseph Panno)*

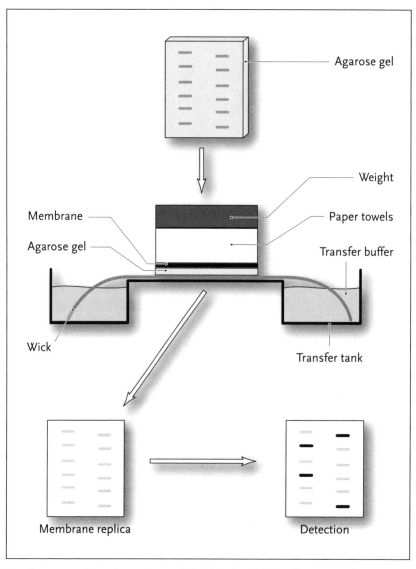

Northern transfer and membrane hybridization. RNA is fractionated on an agarose gel and then placed face down on a paper wick in a transfer tank. The gel is overlaid with a piece of nylon membrane, paper towels, and weight. The paper towels draw the buffer through the gel and the membrane. The flow of buffer elutes the RNA from the gel transferring it to the membrane. A radiolabeled cDNA probe is hybridized to the membrane to detect specific mRNA transcripts. Note that the thickness of the membrane is exaggerated for clarity.

The double-stranded molecule that is formed is a hybrid, being formed between the RNA target, on the membrane, and the DNA probe.

FLUORESCENT IN SITU HYBRIDIZATION (FISH)

Studying gene expression does not always depend on northern blots and filter hybridization. In the 1980s, scientists found that cDNA probes could be hybridized to DNA or mRNA *in situ,* that is, while located within cells or tissue sections fixed on a microscope slide. In this case, the probe is labeled with a fluorescent dye molecule, rather than a radioactive isotope. The samples are then examined and photographed under a fluorescent microscope. FISH is an extremely powerful variation on Southern and northern blots. This procedure gives precise information regarding the identity of a cell that expresses a specific gene, information that usually cannot be obtained with filter hybridization. Organs and tissues are generally composed of many different kinds of cells, which cannot be separated from each other using standard biochemical extraction procedures. Histological sections, however, show clearly the various cell types and, when subjected to FISH analysis, provide clear results as to which cells express specific genes. FISH is also used in clinical laboratories for the diagnosis of genetic abnormalities.

POLYMERASE CHAIN REACTION (PCR)

PCR is simply repetitive DNA replication over a limited, primer-defined region of a suitable template. The region defined by the primers is amplified to such an extent that it can be easily isolated for further study. The reaction exploits the fact that a DNA duplex, in a low-salt buffer, will melt (i.e., separate into two single strands) at 75° C but will reanneal (rehybridize) at 37° C. The reaction is initiated by melting the template in the presence of primers and polymerase in a suitable buffer, cooling quickly to 37° C, and allowing sufficient time for the polymerase to replicate both strands of the template. The temperature is then increased to 75° C to melt the newly formed duplexes and then cooled to 37° C. At the lower temperature, more primer will anneal to initiate another round of replication. The heating-cooling cycle is repeated 20 to 30 times, after which the reaction products are fractionated on an agarose gel and photographed. The band containing the amplified fragment may be cut out of the gel and purified for further study. The DNA polymerase used in these reactions is isolated from thermophilic bacteria that can withstand temperatures of 70° C to 80° C. PCR applications are nearly limitless. It is used to amplify DNA from samples containing, at times, no more than a few cells. It can be used to screen libraries and to identify genes that are turned on or off during embryonic development or during cellular transformation.

GLOSSARY

✖

acetyl   A chemical group derived from acetic acid. Important in energy metabolism and for the modification of proteins.

acetylcholine   A neurotransmitter released at axonal terminals by cholinergic neurons. Found in the central and peripheral nervous system and released at the vertebrate neuromuscular junction.

acetyl-CoA   A water-soluble molecule, coenzyme A (CoA), that carries acetyl groups in cells.

acid   A substance that releases protons when dissolved in water. Carries a net negative charge.

actin filament   A protein filament formed by the polymerization of globular actin molecules. Forms the cytoskeleton of all eukaryotes and part of the contractile apparatus of skeletal muscle.

action potential   A self-propagating electrical impulse that occurs in the membranes of neurons, muscles, photoreceptors, and hair cells of the inner ear.

active transport   Movement of molecules across the cell membrane, utilizing the energy stored in ATP.

adenylate cyclase   A membrane-bound enzyme that catalyzes the conversion of ATP to cyclic AMP. An important component of cell-signaling pathways.

adherens junction   A cell junction in which the cytoplasmic face of the membrane is attached to actin filaments.

adipocyte   A fat cell.

adrenaline (epinephrine)   A hormone released by chromaffin cells in the adrenal gland. Prepares an animal for extreme activity, increases the heart rate and blood-sugar levels.

adult stem cells   Stem cells isolated from adult tissues, such as bone marrow or epithelium.

aerobic   Refers to a process that either requires oxygen or occurs in its presence.

allele   An alternate form of a gene. Diploid organisms have two alleles for each gene, located at the same locus (position) on homologous chromosomes.

allogeneic transplant   A patient receives a tissue or organ transplant from an unrelated individual.

alpha helix   A common folding pattern of proteins in which a linear sequence of amino acids twists into a right-handed helix stabilized by hydrogen bonds.

amino acid   An organic molecule containing amino and carboxyl groups that is a building block of protein.

aminoacyl-tRNA   An amino acid linked by its carboxyl group to a hydroxyl group on tRNA.

aminoacyl-tRNA synthetase   An enzyme that attaches the correct amino acid to a tRNA.

amino terminus   The end of a protein or polypeptide chain that carries a free amino group.

amphipathic   Having both hydrophilic and hydrophobic regions, as in a phospholipid.

anabolism   A collection of metabolic reactions in a cell whereby large molecules are made from smaller ones.

anaerobic   A cellular metabolism that does not depend on molecular oxygen.

anaphase   A mitotic stage in which the two sets of chromosomes move away from each other toward opposite and spindle poles.

anchoring junction   A cell junction that attaches cells to each other.

angiogenesis   Sprouting of new blood vessels from preexisting ones.

angstrom   A unit of length, equal to 10^{-10} meter or 0.1 nanometer (nm), that is used to measure molecules and atoms.

anterior   A position close to or at the head end of the body.

antibiotic   A substance made by bacteria, fungi, and plants that is toxic to microorganisms. Common examples are penicillin and streptomycin.

antibody   A protein made by B cells of the immune system in response to invading microbes.

anticodon A sequence of three nucleotides in tRNA that is complementary to a messenger RNA codon.

antigen A molecule that stimulates an immune response, leading to the formation of antibodies.

antigen-presenting cell A cell of the immune system, such as a monocyte, that presents pieces of an invading microbe (the antigen) to lymphocytes.

antiparallel The relative orientation of the two strands in a DNA double helix; the polarity of one strand is oriented in the opposite direction to the other.

antiporter A membrane carrier protein that transports two different molecules across a membrane in opposite directions.

apoptosis Regulated or programmed form of cell death that may be activated by the cell itself or by the immune system to force cells to commit suicide when they become infected with a virus.

asexual reproduction The process of forming new individuals without gametes or the fertilization of an egg by a sperm. Individuals produced this way are identical to the parent and referred to as a clone.

aster The star-shaped arrangement of microtubules that is characteristic of a mitotic or meiotic spindle.

ATP (adenosine triphosphate) A nucleoside consisting of adenine, ribose, and three phosphate groups that is the main carrier of chemical energy in the cell.

ATPase Any enzyme that catalyzes a biochemical reaction by extracting the necessary energy from ATP.

ATP synthase A protein located in the inner membrane of the mitochondrion that catalyzes the formation of ATP from ADP and inorganic phosphate using the energy supplied by the electron transport chain.

autogeneic transplant A patient receives a transplant of his or her own tissue.

autosome Any chromosome other than a sex chromosome.

axon A long extension of a neuron's cell body that transmits an electrical signal to other neurons.

axonal transport The transport of organelles, such as Golgi vesicles, along an axon to the axonal terminus. Transport also flows from the terminus to the cell body.

bacteria   One of the most ancient forms of cellular life (the other is the Archaea). Bacteria are prokaryotes and some are known to cause disease.

bacterial artificial chromosome (BAC)   A cloning vector that accommodates DNA inserts of up to 1 million base pairs.

bacteriophage   A virus that infects bacteria. Bacteriophages were used to prove that DNA is the cell's genetic material and are now used as cloning vectors.

base   A substance that can accept a proton in solution. The purines and pyrimidines in DNA and RNA are organic bases and are often referred to simply as bases.

base pair   Two nucleotides in RNA or DNA that are held together by hydrogen bonds. Adenine bound to thymine or guanine bound to cytosine are examples of base pairs.

B cell (B lymphocyte)   A white blood cell that makes antibodies and is part of the adaptive immune response.

benign   Tumors that grow to a limited size and do not spread to other parts of the body.

beta sheet   Common structural motif in proteins in which different strands of the protein run alongside each other and are held together by hydrogen bonds.

biopsy   The removal of cells or tissues for examination under a microscope. When only a sample of tissue is removed, the procedure is called an incisional biopsy or core biopsy. When an entire lump or suspicious area is removed, the procedure is called an excisional biopsy. When a sample of tissue or fluid is removed with a needle, the procedure is called a needle biopsy or fine-needle aspiration.

biosphere   The world of living organisms.

bivalent   A duplicated chromosome paired with its homologous duplicated chromosome at the beginning of meiosis.

blastomere   A cell formed by the cleavage of a fertilized egg. Blastomeres are the totipotent cells of the early embryo.

blotting   A technique for transferring DNA (Southern blotting), RNA (northern blotting), or proteins (western blotting) from an agarose or polyacrylamide gel to a nylon membrane.

BRCA1 (breast cancer gene 1)   A gene on chromosome 17 that may be involved in regulating the cell cycle. A person who inherits an altered version of the BRCA1 gene has a higher risk of getting breast, ovarian, or prostate cancer.

BRCA2 (breast cancer gene 2) A gene on chromosome 13 that, when mutated, increases the risk of getting breast, ovarian, or prostate cancer.

budding yeast The common name for the baker's yeast *Saccharomyces cerevisiae,* a popular experimental organism that reproduces by budding off a parental cell.

cadherin Belongs to a family of proteins that mediates cell-to-cell adhesion in animal tissues.

calorie A unit of heat. One calorie is the amount of heat needed to raise the temperature of one gram of water by 1°C. Kilocalories (1,000 calories) are used to describe the energy content of foods.

capsid The protein coat of a virus, formed by auto-assembly of one or more proteins into a geometrically symmetrical structure.

carbohydrate A general class of compounds that includes sugars, containing carbon, hydrogen, and oxygen.

carboxyl group A carbon atom attached to an oxygen and a hydroxyl group.

carboxyl terminus The end of a protein containing a carboxyl group.

carcinogen A compound or form of radiation that can cause cancer.

carcinogenesis The formation of a cancer.

carcinoma Cancer of the epithelium, representing the majority of human cancers.

cardiac muscle Muscle of the heart. Composed of myocytes that are linked together in a communication network based on free passage of small molecules through gap junctions.

caspase A protease involved in the initiation of apoptosis.

catabolism Enzyme-regulated breakdown of large molecules for the extraction of chemical-bond energy. Intermediate products are called catabolites.

catalyst A substance that lowers the activation energy of a reaction.

CD28 Cell-surface protein located in T cell membranes, necessary for the activation of T cells by foreign antigens.

cDNA (complementary DNA) DNA that is synthesized from mRNA, thus containing the complementary sequence. cDNA contains coding sequence but not the regulatory sequences that are present in the genome. Labeled probes are made from cDNA for the study of gene expression.

cell adhesion molecule (CAM)   A cell-surface protein that is used to connect cells to each other.

cell body   The main part of a cell containing the nucleus, Golgi complex, and endoplasmic reticulum. Used in reference to neurons that have long processes (dendrites and axons) extending some distance from the nucleus and cytoplasmic machinery.

cell coat   See **glycocalyx**.

cell-cycle control system   A team of regulatory proteins that governs progression through the cell cycle.

cell-division-cycle gene (*cdc* gene)   A gene that controls a specific step in the cell cycle.

cell fate   The final differentiated state that a pluripotent embryonic cell is expected to attain.

cell-medicated immune response   Activation of specific cells to launch an immune response against an invading microbe.

cell nuclear replacement   Animal-cloning technique whereby a somatic cell nucleus is transferred to an enucleated oocyte. Synonomous with somatic-cell nuclear transfer.

central nervous system (CNS)   That part of a nervous system that analyzes signals from the body and the environment. In animals, the CNS includes the brain and spinal cord.

centriole   A cylindrical array of microtubules that is found at the center of a centrosome in animal cells.

centromere   A region of a mitotic chromosome that holds sister chromatids together. Microtubules of the spindle fiber connect to an area of the centromere called the kinetochore.

centrosome   Organizes the mitotic spindle and the spindle poles. In most animal cells it contains a pair of centrioles.

chiasma (plural chiasmata)   An X-shaped connection between homologous chromosomes that occurs during meiosis I, representing a site of crossing-over, or genetic exchange between the two chromosomes.

chromatid   A duplicate chromosome that is still connected to the original at the centromere. The identical pair are called sister chromatids.

chromatin   A complex of DNA and proteins (histones and nonhistones) that forms each chromosome and is found in the nucleus of all eukaryotes. Decondensed and threadlike during interphase.

chromatin condensation   Compaction of different regions of interphase chromosomes that is mediated by the histones.

chromosome   One long molecule of DNA that contains the organism's genes. In prokaryotes, the chromosome is circular and naked; in eukaryotes, it is linear and complexed with histone and nonhistone proteins.

chromosome condensation   Compaction of entire chromosomes in preparation for cell division.

clinical breast exam   An exam of the breast performed by a physician to check for lumps or other changes.

cyclic adenosine monophosphate (cAMP)   A second messenger in a cell-signaling pathway that is produced from ATP by the enzyme adenylate cyclase.

cyclin   A protein that activates protein kinases (cyclin-dependent protein kinases, or Cdk) that control progression from one state of the cell cycle to another.

cytochemistry   The study of the intracellular distribution of chemicals.

cytochrome   Colored, iron-containing protein that is part of the electron transport chain.

cytotoxic T cell   A T lymphocyte that kills infected body cells.

dendrite   An extension of a nerve cell that receives signals from other neurons.

dexrazoxane   A drug used to protect the heart from the toxic effects of anthracycline drugs such as doxorubicin. It belongs to the family of drugs called chemoprotective agents.

dideoxy sequencing   A method for sequencing DNA that employs dideoxyribose nucleotides.

diploid   A genetic term meaning two sets of homologous chromosomes, one set from the mother and the other from the father. Thus diploid organisms have two versions (alleles) of each gene in the genome.

DNA (deoxyribonucleic acid)   A long polymer formed by linking four different kinds of nucleotides together like beads on a string. The sequence of nucleotides is used to encode an organism's genes.

DNA helicase An enzyme that separates and unwinds the two DNA strands in preparation for replication or transcription.

DNA library A collection of DNA fragments that are cloned into plasmids or viral genomes.

DNA ligase An enzyme that joins two DNA strands together to make a continuous DNA molecule.

DNA microarray A technique for studying the simultaneous expression of a very large number of genes.

DNA polymerase An enzyme that synthesizes DNA using one strand as a template.

DNA primase An enzyme that synthesizes a short strand of RNA that serves as a primer for DNA replication.

dorsal The backside of an animal. Also refers to the upper surface of anatomical structures, such as arms or wings.

dorsoventral The body axis running from the backside to the frontside or the upperside to the underside of a structure.

double helix The three-dimensional structure of DNA in which the two strands twist around each other to form a spiral.

doxorubicin An anticancer drug that belongs to a family of antitumor antibiotics.

Drosophila melanogaster Small species of fly, commonly called a fruit fly, that is used as an experimental organism in genetics, embryology, and gerontology.

ductal carcinoma in situ (DCIS) Abnormal cells that involve only the lining of a breast duct. The cells have not spread outside the duct to other tissues in the breast. Also called intraductal carcinoma.

dynein A motor protein that is involved in chromosome movements during cell division.

dysplasia Disordered growth of cells in a tissue or organ, often leading to the development of cancer.

ectoderm An embryonic tissue that is the precursor of the epidermis and the nervous system.

electrochemical gradient A differential concentration of an ion or molecule across the cell membrane that serves as a source of potential energy and may polarize the cell electrically.

electron microscope A microscope that uses electrons to produce a high-resolution image of the cell.

embryogensis The development of an embryo from a fertilized egg.

embryonic stem cell (ES cell) A pluripotent cell derived from the inner cell mass (the cells that give rise to the embryo instead of the placenta) of a mammalian embryo.

endocrine cell A cell that is specialized for the production and release of hormones. Such cells make up hormone-producing tissue such as the pituitary gland or gonads.

endocytosis Cellular uptake of material from the environment by invagination of the cell membrane to form a vesicle called an endosome. The endosome's contents are made available to the cell after it fuses with a lysosome.

endoderm An embryonic tissue layer that gives rise to the gut.

endoplasmic reticulum (ER) Membrane-bounded chambers that are used to modify newly synthesized proteins with the addition of sugar molecules (glycosylation). When finished, the glycosylated proteins are sent to the Golgi apparatus in exocytotic vesicles.

endothelial cell A cell that forms the endothelium, a thin sheet of cells lining the inner surface of all blood vessels.

enhancer A DNA regulatory sequence that provides a binding site for transcription factors capable of increasing the rate of transcription for a specific gene. Often located thousands of base pairs away from the gene it regulates.

enveloped virus A virus containing a capsid that is surrounded by a lipid bilayer originally obtained from the membrane of a previously infected cell.

enzyme A protein or RNA that catalyzes a specific chemical reaction.

epidermis The epithelial layer, or skin, that covers the outer surface of the body.

ER signal sequence The amino terminal sequence that directs proteins to enter the endoplasmic reticulum (ER). This sequence is removed once the protein enters the ER.

erythrocyte A red blood cell that contains the oxygen-carrying pigment hemoglobin used to deliver oxygen to cells in the body.

***Escherichia coli* (*E. coli*)** Rod shape, gram negative bacterium that inhabits the intestinal tract of most animals and is used as an experimental organism by geneticists and biomedical researchers.

euchromatin   Lightly staining portion of interphase chromatin, in contrast to the darkly staining heterochromatin (condensed chromatin). Euchromatin contains most, if not all, of the active genes.

eukaryote (eucaryote)   A cell containing a nucleus and many membrane-bounded organelles. All life-forms, except bacteria and viruses, are composed of eukaryote cells.

exocytosis   The process by which molecules are secreted from a cell. Molecules to be secreted are located in Golgi-derived vesicles that fuse with the inner surface of the cell membrane, depositing the contents into the intercellular space.

exon   Coding region of a eukaryote gene that is represented in messenger RNA, and thus directs the synthesis of a specific protein.

expression studies   Examination of the type and quantity of mRNA or protein that is produced by cells, tissues, or organs.

fat   A lipid material, consisting of triglycerides (fatty acids bound to glycerol), that is stored in adipocytes as an energy reserve.

fatty acid   A compound that has a carboxylic acid attached to a long hydrocarbon chain. A major source of cellular energy and a component of phospholipids.

fertilization   The fusion of haploid male and female gametes to form a diploid zygote.

fibroblast   The cell type that, by secreting an extracellular matrix, gives rise to the connective tissue of the body.

filter hybridization   The detection of specific DNA or RNA molecules, fixed on a nylon filter, by incubating the filter with a labelled probe that hybridizes to the target sequence.

fixative   A chemical that is used to preserve cells and tissues. Common examples are formaldehyde, methanol, and acetic acid.

flagellum (plural flagella)   Whiplike structure found in prokaryotes and eukaryotes that are used to propel cells through water.

fluorescein   Fluorescent dye that produces a green light when illuminated with ultraviolet or blue light.

fluorescent dye   A dye that absorbs UV or blue light and emits light of a longer wavelength, usually as green or red light.

fluorescent microscope   A microscope that is equipped with special filters and a beam splitter for the examination of tissues and cells stained with a fluorescent dye.

follicle cell Cells that surround and help feed a developing oocyte.

G_0 G "zero" refers to a phase of the cell cycle. State of withdrawal from the cycle as the cell enters a resting or quiescent stage. Occurs in differentiated body cells as well as developing oocytes.

G_1 Gap 1 refers to the phase of the cell cycle that occurs just after mitosis and before the next round of DNA synthesis.

G_2 Gap 2 refers to the phase of the cell cycle that follows DNA replication and precedes mitosis.

gap junction A communication channel in the membranes of adjacent cells that allows free passage of ions and small molecules.

gastrulation An embryological event in which a spherical embryo is converted into an elongated structure with a head end, a tail end, and a gut (gastrula).

gene A region of the DNA that specifies a specific protein or RNA molecule that is handed down from one generation to the next. This region includes both the coding, noncoding, and regulatory sequences.

gene regulatory protein Any protein that binds to DNA and thereby affects the expression of a specific gene.

gene repressor protein A protein that binds to DNA and blocks transcription of a specific gene.

gene therapy A method for treating disease whereby a defective gene, causing the disease, is either repaired, replaced, or supplemented with a functional copy.

genetic code A set of rules that assigns a specific DNA or RNA triplet, consisting of a three-base sequence, to a specific amino acid.

genome All of the genes that belong to a cell or an organism.

genomic library A collection of DNA fragments, obtained by digesting genomic DNA with a restriction enzyme, that are cloned into plasmid or viral vectors.

genomics The study of DNA sequences and their role in the function and structure of an organism.

genotype The genetic composition of a cell or organism.

germ cell Cells that develop into gametes, either sperm or oocytes.

glucose Six-carbon monosaccharide (sugar) that is the principal source of energy for many cells and organisms. Stored as glycogen in animal cells and as starch in plants. Wood is an elaborate polymer of glucose and other sugars.

glycerol   A three-carbon alcohol that is an important component of phospholipids.

glycocalyx   A molecular "forest," consisting of glycosylated proteins and lipids, that covers the surface of every cell. The glycoproteins and glycolipids, carried to the cell membrane by Golgi-derived vesicles, have many functions, including the formation of ion channels, cell-signaling receptors and transporters.

glycogen   A polymer of glucose used to store energy in an animal cell.

glycolysis   The degradation of glucose with production of ATP.

glycoprotein   Any protein that has a chain of glucose molecules (oligosaccharide) attached to some of the amino acid residues.

glycosylation   The process of adding one or more sugar molecules to proteins or lipids.

glycosyl transferase   An enzyme in the Golgi complex that adds glucose to proteins.

Golgi complex (Golgi apparatus)   Membrane-bounded organelle in eukaryote cells that receives glycoproteins from the ER, which are modified and sorted before being sent to their final destination. The Golgi complex is also the source of glycolipids that are destined for the cell membrane. The glycoproteins and glycolipids leave the Golgi by exocytosis. This organelle is named after the Italian histologist Camillo Golgi, who discovered it in 1898.

granulocyte   A type of white blood cell that includes the neutrophils, basophils, and eosinophils.

growth factor   A small protein (polypeptide) that can stimulate cells to grow and proliferate.

haploid   Having only one set of chromosomes. A condition that is typical in gametes, such as sperm and eggs.

HeLa cell   A tumor-derived cell line, originally isolated from a cancer patient in 1951. Currently used by many laboratories to study the cell biology of cancer and carcinogenesis.

helix-loop-helix   A structural motif common to a group of gene regulatory proteins.

helper T cell   A type of T lymphocyte that helps stimulate B cells to make antibodies directed against a specific microbe or antigen.

hemoglobin   An iron-containing protein complex, located in red blood cells that picks up oxygen in the lungs and carries it to other tissues and cells of the body.

hemopoiesis   Production of blood cells, occurring primarily in the bone marrow.

hepatocyte   A liver cell.

heterochromatin   A region of a chromosome that is highly condensed and transcriptionally inactive.

histochemistry   The study of chemical differentiation of tissues.

histology   The study of tissues.

histone   Small nuclear proteins, rich in the amino acids arginine and lysine, that form the nucleosome in eukaryote nuclei, a beadlike structure that is a major component of chromatin.

HIV   The human immunodeficiency virus that is responsible for AIDS.

homolog   One of two or more genes that have a similar sequence and are descended from a common ancestor gene.

homologous   Organs or molecules that are similar in structure because they have descended from a common ancestor. Used primarily in reference to DNA and protein sequences.

homologous chromosomes   Two copies of the same chromosome, one inherited from the mother and the other from the father.

hormone   A signaling molecule, produced and secreted by endocrine glands. Usually released into general circulation for coordination of an animal's physiology.

housekeeping gene   A gene that codes for a protein that is needed by all cells, regardless of the cell's specialization. Genes encoding enzymes involved in glycolysis and the Krebs cycle are common examples.

hybridization   A term used in molecular biology (recombinant DNA technology) meaning the formation of a double-stranded nucleic acid through complementary base-pairing. A property that is exploited in filter hybridization, a procedure that is used to screen gene libraries and to study gene structure and expression.

hydrophilic   A polar compound that mixes readily with water.

hydrophobic   A nonpolar molecule that dissolves in fat and lipid solutions but not in water.

hydroxyl group (-OH) Chemical group consisting of oxygen and hydrogen that is a prominent part of alcohol.

image analysis A computerized method for extracting information from digitized microscopic images of cells or cell organelles.

immunofluorescence Detection of a specific cellular protein with the aid of a fluorescent dye that is coupled to an antibody.

immunoglobulin (Ig) An antibody made by B cells as part of the adaptive immune response.

incontinence Inability to control the flow of urine from the bladder (urinary incontinence) or the escape of stool from the rectum (fecal incontinence).

in situ hybridization A method for studying gene expression, whereby a labeled cDNA or RNA probe hybridizes to a specific mRNA in intact cells or tissues. The procedure is usually carried out on tissue sections or smears of individual cells.

insulin Polypeptide hormone secreted by β (beta) cells in the vertebrate pancreas. Production of this hormone is regulated directly by the amount of glucose that is in the blood.

interleukin A small protein hormone, secreted by lymphocytes, to activate and coordinate the adaptive immune response.

interphase The period between each cell division, which includes the G_1, S, and G_2 phases of the cell cycle.

intron A section of a eukaryotic gene that is noncoding. It is transcribed, but does not appear in the mature mRNA.

in vitro Refers to cells growing in culture, or a biochemical reaction occurring in a test tube (Latin for "in glass").

in vivo A biochemical reaction, or a process, occurring in living cells or a living organism (Latin for "in life").

ion An atom that has gained or lost electrons, thus acquiring a charge. Common examples are Na^+ and Ca^{++} ions.

ion channel A transmembrane channel that allows ions to diffuse across the membrane and down their electrochemical gradient.

Jak-STAT signaling pathway One of several cell-signaling pathways that activates gene expression. The pathway is activated through cell-surface receptors and cytoplasmic Janus kinases (Jaks), and signal transducers and activators of transcription (STATs).

karyotype   A pictorial catalog of a cell's chromosomes, showing their number, size, shape, and overall banding pattern.

keratin   Proteins produced by specialized epithelial cells called keratinocytes. Keratin is found in hair, fingernails, and feathers.

kinesin   A motor protein that uses energy obtained from the hydrolysis of ATP to move along a microtubule.

kinetochore   A complex of proteins that forms around the centromere of mitotic or meiotic chromosomes, providing an attachment site for microtubules. The other end of each microtubule is attached to a chromosome.

Krebs cycle (citric acid cycle)   The central metabolic pathway in all eukaryotes and aerobic prokaryotes, discovered by the German chemist Hans Krebs in 1937. The cycle oxidizes acetyl groups derived from food molecules. The end products are CO_2, H_2O, and high-energy electrons, which pass via NADH and FADH2 to the respiratory chain. In eukaryotes, the Krebs cycle is located in the mitochondria.

labeling reaction   The addition of a radioactive atom or fluorescent dye to DNA or RNA for use as a probe in filter hybridization.

lagging strand   One of the two newly synthesized DNA strands at a replication fork. The lagging strand is synthesized discontinuously, and therefore, its completion lags behind the second, or leading, strand.

lambda bacteriophage   A viral parasite that infects bacteria. Widely used as a DNA cloning vector.

leading strand   One of the two newly synthesized DNA strands at a replication fork. The leading strand is made by continuous synthesis in the 5' to 3' direction.

leucine zipper   A structural motif of DNA binding proteins, in which two identical proteins are joined together at regularly spaced leucine residues, much like a zipper, to form a dimer.

leukemia   Cancer of white blood cells.

lipid bilayer   Two closely aligned sheets of phospholipids that form the core structure of all cell membranes. The two layers are aligned such that the hydrophobic tails are interior, while the hydrophilic head groups are exterior on both surfaces.

liposome   An artificial lipid bilayer vesicle used in membrane studies and as an artificial gene therapy vector.

locus   A term from genetics that refers to the position of a gene along a chromosome. Different alleles of the same gene occupy the same locus.

long-term potentiation (LTP)   A physical remodeling of synaptic junctions that receive continuous stimulation.

lymphocyte   A type of white blood cell that is involved in the adaptive immune response. There are two kinds of lymphocytes: T lymphocytes and B lymphocytes. T lymphocytes (T cells) mature in the thymus and attack invading microbes directly. B lymphocytes (B cells) mature in the bone marrow and make antibodies that are designed to immobilize or destroy specific microbes or antigens.

lysis   The rupture of the cell membrane followed by death of the cell.

lysosome   Membrane-bounded organelle of eukaryotes that contains powerful digestive enzymes.

macromolecule   A very large molecule that is built from smaller molecular subunits. Common examples are DNA, proteins, and polysaccharides.

magnetic resonance imaging (MRI)   A procedure in which radio waves and a powerful magnet linked to a computer are used to create detailed pictures of areas inside the body. These pictures can show the difference between normal and diseased tissue. MRI makes better images of organs and soft tissue than other scanning techniques, such as CT or X-ray. MRI is especially useful for imaging the brain, spine, the soft tissue of joints, and the inside of bones. Also called nuclear magnetic resonance imaging.

major histocompatibility complex   Vertebrate genes that code for a large family of cell-surface glycoproteins that bind foreign antigens and present them to T cells to induce an immune response.

malignant   Refers to the functional status of a cancer cell that grows aggressively and is able to metastasize, or colonize, other areas of the body.

mammography   The use of X-rays to create a picture of the breast.

MAP-kinase (mitogen-activated protein kinase)   A protein kinase that is part of a cell-proliferation-inducing signaling pathway.

M-cyclin   A eukaryote enzyme that regulates mitosis.

meiosis   A special form of cell division by which haploid gametes are produced. This is accomplished with two rounds of cell division but only one round of DNA replication.

melanocyte   A skin cell that produces the pigment melanin.

membrane   The lipid bilayer, and the associated glycocalyx, that surrounds and encloses all cells.

membrane channel   A protein complex that forms a pore or channel through the membrane for the free passage of ions and small molecules.

membrane potential   A buildup of charged ions on one side of the cell membrane establishes an electrochemical gradient that is measured in millivolts (mV). An important characteristic of neurons as it provides the electric current, when ion channels open, that enable these cells to communicate with each other.

mesoderm   An embryonic germ layer that gives rise to muscle, connective tissue, bones, and many internal organs.

messenger RNA (mRNA)   An RNA transcribed from a gene that is used as the gene template by the ribosomes, and other components of the translation machinery, to synthesize a protein.

metabolism   The sum total of the chemical processes that occur in living cells.

metaphase   The stage of mitosis at which the chromosomes are attached to the spindle but have not begun to move apart.

metaphase plate   Refers to the imaginary plane established by the chromosomes as they line up at right angles to the spindle poles.

metaplasia   A change in the pattern of cellular behavior that often precedes the development of cancer.

metastasis   Spread of cancer cells from the site of the original tumor to other parts of the body.

methyl group (-CH$_3$)   Hydrophobic chemical group derived from methane. Occurs at the end of a fatty acid.

micrograph   Photograph taken through a light, or electron, microscope.

micrometer (μm or micron)   Equal to 10^{-6} meters.

microtubule   A fine cylindrical tube made of the protein tubulin, forming a major component of the eukaryote cytoskeleton.

millimeter (mm)   Equal to 10^{-3} meters.

mitochondrion (plural mitochondria)   Eukaryote organelle, formerly free-living, that produces most of the cell's ATP.

mitogen   A hormone or signaling molecule that stimulates cells to grow and divide.

mitosis   Division of a eukaryotic nucleus. From the Greek *mitos,* meaning "a thread," in reference to the threadlike appearance of interphase chromosomes.

mitotic chromosome   Highly condensed duplicated chromosomes held together by the centromere. Each member of the pair is referred to as a sister chromatid.

mitotic spindle   Array of microtubules, fanning out from the polar centrioles and connecting to each of the chromosomes.

molecule   Two or more atoms linked together by covalent bonds.

monoclonal antibody   An antibody produced from a B cell–derived clonal line. Since all of the cells are clones of the original B cell, the antibodies produced are identical.

monocyte   A type of white blood cell that is involved in the immune response.

motif   An element of structure or pattern that may be a recurring domain in a variety of proteins.

M phase   The period of the cell cycle (mitosis or meiosis) when the chromosomes separate and migrate to the opposite poles of the spindle.

multipass transmembrane protein   A membrane protein that passes back and forth across the lipid bilayer.

mutant   A genetic variation within a population.

mutation   A heritable change in the nucleotide sequence of a chromosome.

myelin sheath   Insulation applied to the axons of neurons. The sheath is produced by oligodendrocytes in the central nervous system and by Schwann cells in the peripheral nervous system.

myeloid cell   White blood cells other than lymphocytes.

myoblast   Muscle precursor cell. Many myoblasts fuse into a syncytium, containing many nuclei, to form a single muscle cell.

myocyte   A muscle cell.

NAD (nicotine adenine dinucleotide)   Accepts a hydride ion (H^-), produced by the Krebs cycle, forming NADH, the main carrier of electrons for oxidative phosphorylation.

NADH dehydrogenase Removes electrons from NADH and passes them down the electron transport chain.

nanometer (nm) Equal to 10^{-9} meters or 10^{-3} microns.

natural killer cell (NK cell) A lymphocyte that kills virus-infected cells in the body. It also kills foreign cells associated with a tissue or organ transplant.

neuromuscular junction A special form of synapse between a motor neuron and a skeletal muscle cell.

neuron A cell specially adapted for communication that forms the nervous system of all animals.

neurotransmitter A chemical released by neurons at a synapse that transmits a signal to another neuron.

non-small-cell lung cancer A group of lung cancers that includes squamous cell carcinoma, adenocarcinoma, and large cell carcinoma. The small cells are endocrine cells.

northern blotting A technique for the study of gene expression. Messenger RNA (mRNA) is fractionated on an agarose gel and then transferred to a piece of nylon filter paper (or membrane). A specific mRNA is detected by hybridization with a labeled DNA or RNA probe. The original blotting technique invented by E. M. Southern inspired the name.

nuclear envelope The double membrane (two lipid bilayers) enclosing the cell nucleus.

nuclear localization signal (NLS) A short amino acid sequence located on proteins that are destined for the cell nucleus after they are translated in the cytoplasm.

nucleic acid DNA or RNA, a macromolecule consisting of a chain of nucleotides.

nucleolar organizer Region of a chromosome containing a cluster of ribosomal RNA genes that gives rise to the nucleolus.

nucleolus A structure in the nucleus where ribosomal RNA is transcribed and ribosomal subunits are assembled.

nucleoside A purine or pyrimidine linked to a ribose or deoxyribose sugar.

nucleosome A beadlike structure, consisting of histone proteins.

nucleotide A nucleoside containing one or more phosphate groups linked to the 5' carbon of the ribose sugar. DNA and RNA are nucleotide polymers.

nucleus Eukaryote cell organelle that contains the DNA genome on one or more chromosomes.

oligodendrocyte A myelinating glia cell of the vertebrate central nervous system.

oligo labeling A method for incorporating labeled nucleotides into a short piece of DNA or RNA. Also known as the random-primer labeling method.

oligomer A short polymer, usually consisting of amino acids (oligopeptides), sugars (oligosaccharides), or nucleotides (oligonucleotides). Taken from the Greek word *oligos,* meaning "few" or "little."

oncogene A mutant form of a normal cellular gene, known as a proto-oncogene, that can transform a cell to a cancerous phenotype.

oocyte A female gamete or egg cell.

operator A region of a prokaryote chromosome that controls the expression of adjacent genes.

operon Two or more prokaryote genes that are transcribed into a single mRNA.

organelle A membrane-bounded structure, occurring in eukaryote cells, that has a specialized function. Examples are the nucleus, Golgi complex, and endoplasmic reticulum.

osmosis The movement of solvent across a semipermeable membrane that separates a solution with a high concentration of solutes from one with a low concentration of solutes. The membrane must be permeable to the solvent but not to the solutes. In the context of cellular osmosis, the solvent is always water, the solutes are ions and molecules, and the membrane is the cell membrane.

osteoblast Cells that form bones.

ovulation Rupture of a mature follicle with subsequent release of a mature oocyte from the ovary.

oxidative phosphorylation Generation of high-energy electrons from food molecules that are used to power the synthesis of ATP from ADP and inorganic phosphate. The electrons are eventually transferred to oxygen to complete the process. Occurs in bacteria and mitochondria.

p53 A tumor-suppressor gene that is mutated in about half of all human cancers. The normal function of the *p53* protein is to block passage through the cell cycle when DNA damage is detected.

parthenogenesis   A natural form of animal cloning whereby an individual is produced without the formation of haploid gametes and the fertilization of an egg.

pathogen   An organism that causes disease.

PCR (polymerase chain reaction)   A method for amplifying specific regions of DNA by temperature cycling a reaction mixture containing the template, a heat-stable DNA polymerase, and replication primers.

peptide bond   The chemical bond that links amino acids together to form a protein.

pH   Measures the acidity of a solution as a negative logarithmic function (p) of H^+ concentration (H). Thus a pH of 2.0 (10^{-2} molar H^+) is acidic, whereas a pH of 8.0 (10^{-8} molar H^+) is basic.

phagocyte   A cell that engulfs other cells or debris by phagocytosis.

phagocytosis   A process whereby cells engulf other cells or organic material by endocytosis. A common practice among protozoans and cells of the vertebrate immune system. (Derived from the Greek word *phagein*, "to eat.")

phenotype   Physical characteristics of a cell or organism.

phospholipid   The kind of lipid molecule used to construct cell membranes. Composed of a hydrophilic head-group, phosphate, glycerol, and two hydrophobic fatty acid tails.

phosphorylation   A chemical reaction in which a phosphate is covalently bonded to another molecule.

photoreceptor   A molecule or cell that responds to light.

photosynthesis   A biochemical process in which plants, algae, and certain bacteria use energy obtained from sunlight to synthesize macromolecules from CO_2 and H_2O.

phylogeny   The evolutionary history of an organism, or group of organisms, often represented diagrammatically as a phylogenetic tree.

pinocytosis   A form of endocytosis whereby fluid is brought into the cell from the environment.

placebo   An inactive substance that looks the same, and is administered in the same way, as a drug in a clinical trial.

plasmid   A minichromosome, often carrying antibiotic-resistant genes, that occurs naturally among prokaryotes. Used extensively as a DNA cloning vector.

platelet   A cell fragment, derived from megakaryocytes and lacking a nucleus, that is present in the bloodstream and is involved in blood coagulation.

ploidy   The total number of chromosomes (n) that a cell has. Ploidy is also measured as the amount of DNA (C) in a given cell relative to a haploid nucleus of the same organism. Most organisms are diploid, having two sets of chromosomes, one from each parent, but there is great variation among plants and animals. The silk gland of the moth *Bombyx mori,* for example, has cells that are extremely polyploid, reaching values of 100,000C. Flowers are often highly polyploid, and vertebrate hepatocytes may be 16C.

point mutation   A change in DNA, particularly in a region containing a gene, that alters a single nucleotide.

polyploid   Possessing more than two sets of homologous chromosomes.

portal system   A system of liver vessels that carries liver enzymes directly to the digestive tract.

probe   Usually a fragment of a cloned DNA molecule that is labeled with a radioisotope or fluorescent dye and used to detect specific DNA or RNA molecules on Southern or northern blots.

promoter   A DNA sequence to which RNA polymerase binds to initiate gene transcription.

prophase   The first stage of mitosis. The chromosomes are duplicated and beginning to condense but are attached to the spindle.

protein   A major constituent of cells and organisms. Proteins, made by linking amino acids together, are used for structural purposes and regulate many biochemical reactions in their alternative role as enzymes. Proteins range in size from just a few amino acids to more than 200.

protein glycosylation   The addition of sugar molecules to a protein.

proto-oncogene   A normal gene that can be converted to a cancer-causing gene (oncogene) by a point mutation or through inappropriate expression.

protozoa   Free-living, single-cell eukaryotes that feed on bacteria and other microorganisms. Common examples are *Paramecium* and *Amoeba.* Parasitic forms are also known that inhabit the digestive and urogenital tract of many animals, including humans.

purine A nitrogen-containing compound that is found in RNA and DNA. Two examples are adenine and guanine.

pyrimidine A nitrogen-containing compound found in RNA and DNA. Examples are cytosine, thymine, and uracil (RNA only).

radioactive isotope An atom with an unstable nucleus that emits radiation as it decays.

randomized clinical trial A study in which the participants are assigned by chance to separate groups that compare different treatments; neither the researchers nor the participants can choose which group. Using chance to assign people to groups means that the groups will be similar and that the treatments they receive can be compared objectively. At the time of the trial, it is not known which treatment is best.

reagent A chemical solution designed for a specific biochemical or histochemical procedure.

recombinant DNA A DNA molecule that has been formed by joining two or more fragments from different sources.

regulatory sequence A DNA sequence to which proteins bind that regulate the assembly of the transcriptional machinery.

replication bubble Local dissociation of the DNA double helix in preparation for replication. Each bubble contains two replication forks.

replication fork The Y-shaped region of a replicating chromosome. Associated with replication bubbles.

replication origin (origin of replication, ORI) The location at which DNA replication begins.

respiratory chain (electron transport chain) A collection of iron- and copper-containing proteins, located in the inner mitochondrion membrane, that utilize the energy of electrons traveling down the chain to synthesize ATP.

restriction enzyme An enzyme that cuts DNA at specific sites.

restriction map The size and number of DNA fragments obtained after digesting with one or more restriction enzymes.

retrovirus A virus that converts its RNA genome to DNA once it has infected a cell.

reverse transcriptase An RNA-dependent DNA polymerase. This enzyme synthesizes DNA by using RNA as a template, the reverse of the usual flow of genetic information from DNA to RNA.

ribosomal RNA (rRNA)   RNA that is part of the ribosome and serves both a structural and functional role, possibly by catalyzing some of the steps involved in protein synthesis.

ribosome   A complex of protein and RNA that catalyzes the synthesis of proteins.

rough endoplasmic reticulum (rough ER)   Endoplasmic reticulum that has ribosomes bound to its outer surface.

Saccharomyces   Genus of budding yeast that are frequently used in the study of eukaryote cell biology.

sarcoma   Cancer of connective tissue.

Schwann cell   Glia cell that produces myelin in the peripheral nervous system.

screening   Checking for disease when there are no symptoms.

senescence   Physical and biochemical changes that occur in cells and organisms with age.

signal transduction   A process by which a signal is relayed to the interior of a cell where it elicits a response at the cytoplasmic or nuclear level.

smooth muscle cell   Muscles lining the intestinal tract and arteries. Lacks the striations typical of cardiac and skeletal muscle, giving it a smooth appearance when viewed under a microscope.

somatic cell   Any cell in a plant or animal except those that produce gametes (germ cells or germ cell precursors).

somatic cell nuclear transfer   Animal cloning technique whereby a somatic cell nucleus is transferred to an enucleated oocyte. Synonomous with cell nuclear replacement.

Southern blotting   The transfer of DNA fragments from an agarose gel to a piece of nylon filter paper. Specific fragments are identified by hybridizing the filter to a labeled probe. Invented by the Scottish scientist E. M. Southern in 1975.

stem cell   Pluripotent progenitor cell, found in embryos and various parts of the body, that can differentiate into a wide variety of cell types.

steroid   A hydrophobic molecule with a characteristic four-ringed structure. Sex hormones, such as estrogen and testosterone, are steroids.

structural gene A gene that codes for a protein or an RNA. Distinguished from regions of the DNA that are involved in regulating gene expression but are noncoding.

synapse A neural communication junction between an axon and a dendrite. Signal transmission occurs when neurotransmitters, released into the junction by the axon of one neuron, stimulate receptors on the dendrite of a second neuron.

syncytium A large multinucleated cell. Skeletal muscle cells are syncytiums produced by the fusion of many myoblasts.

syngeneic transplants A patient receives tissue or an organ from an identical twin.

tamoxifen A drug that is used to treat breast cancer. Tamoxifen blocks the effects of the hormone estrogen in the body. It belongs to the family of drugs called antiestrogens.

T cell (T lymphocyte) A white blood cell involved in activating and coordinating the immune response.

telomere The end of a chromosome. Replaced by the enzyme telomerase with each round of cell division to prevent shortening of the chromosomes.

telophase The final stage of mitosis in which the chromosomes decondense and the nuclear envelope reforms.

template A single strand of DNA or RNA whose sequence serves as a guide for the synthesis of a complementary, or daughter, strand.

therapeutic cloning The cloning of a human embryo for the purpose of harvesting the inner cell mass (ES cells).

topoisomerase An enzyme that makes reversible cuts in DNA to relieve strain or to undo knots.

transcription The copying of a DNA sequence into RNA, catalyzed by RNA polymerase.

transcriptional factor A general term referring to a wide assortment of proteins needed to initiate or regulate transcription.

transfection Introduction of a foreign gene into a eukaryote cell.

transfer RNA (tRNA) A collection of small RNA molecules that transfer an amino acid to a growing polypeptide chain on a ribosome. There is a separate tRNA for amino acid.

transgenic organism A plant or animal that has been transfected with a foreign gene.

trans-Golgi network   The membrane surfaces where glycoproteins and glycolipids exit the Golgi complex in transport vesicles.

translation   A ribosome-catalyzed process whereby the nucleotide sequence of an mRNA is used as a template to direct the synthesis of a protein.

transposable element (transposon)   A segment of DNA that can move from one region of a genome to another.

ultrasound (ultrasonography)   A procedure in which high-energy sound waves (ultrasound) are bounced off internal tissues or organs producing echoes that are used to form a picture of body tissues (a sonogram).

umbilical cord blood stem cells   Stem cells, produced by a human fetus and the placenta, that are found in the blood that passes from the placenta to the fetus.

vector   A virus or plasmid used to carry a DNA fragment into a bacterial cell (for cloning) or into a eukaryote to produce a transgenic organism.

vesicle   A membrane-bounded bubble found in eukaryote cells. Vesicles carry material from the ER to the Golgi and from the Golgi to the cell membrane.

virus   A particle containing an RNA or DNA genome surrounded by a protein coat. Viruses are cellular parasites that cause many diseases.

western blotting   The transfer of protein from a polyacrylamide gel to a piece of nylon filter paper. Specific proteins are detected with labeled antibodies. The name was inspired by the original blotting technique invented by E. M. Southern.

yeast   Common term for unicellular eukaryotes that are used to brew beer and make bread. Bakers yeast, *Saccharomyces cerevisiae,* is also widely used in studies on cell biology.

zygote   A diploid cell produced by the fusion of a sperm and egg.

FURTHER READING

ɔc

Access Excellence, The National Health Museum. Washington, DC, U.S.A. "Structure of DNA." Available online. URL:www.access. excellence.org/AB/GG/structure.html. Accessed on February 20, 2004.

Alberts, Bruce. *Essential Cell Biology.* New York: Garland Publishing, 1998.

"Astroglia Induce Neurogenesis From Adult Neural Stem Cells." *Nature* 417 (2002): 39–44. This research paper is directed at professional scientists but is recommended to beginning students for the beautiful fluorescent images of neurons growing in culture.

Cook-Deegan, R. *The Gene Wars: Science, Politics, and the Human Genome.* New York: W. W. Norton, 1994.

De Kruif, Paul. *Microbe Hunters.* New York: Harcourt, Brace, 1926.

"Double Helix: 50 Years of DNA." Many articles assembled by the journal *Nature* to commemorate the 50th anniversary of James Watson and Francis Crick's classic paper describing the structure of DNA. Available online. URL: http://www.nature.com/nature/dna50/index. html. Accessed on October 9, 2003.

Dynamic Development. University of Calgary, Alberta, Canada. "Historical Roots of Developmental Biology." Available online. URL: http://www.ucalgary.ca./~browder/roots.html. Accessed on February 20, 2004.

Food and Drug Administration. Rockville MD, U.S.A. "Bad Bug Book." This handbook provides basic facts regarding pathogenic microorganisms and natural toxins. The information comes from the Food & Drug Administration, the Centers for Disease Control & Prevention, the USDA Food Safety Inspection Service, and the National Institutes of Health. Available online. URL: http://vm.cfsan.fda.gov/ ~mow/intro.html. Accessed on February 20, 2004.

Genetic Science Learning Center. University of Utah, U.S.A. "Human Genetics." Available online. URL: http://gslc.genetics.utah.edu. Accessed on February 20, 2004.

Greenreef. "Reef Briefs." A collection of articles about reef ecology. Green Reef is a nonprofit scientific and educational organization that promotes interest in wildlife and conservation of natural resources. Available online. URL: http://www.greenreefbelize.com/reefbriefs/index.html. Accessed on February 20, 2004.

"Human Genome: A Low Number Wins the GeneSweep Pool." *Science,* June 6, 2003. Available online. URL: http://www.science.com. Accessed on October 9, 2003.

Institute of Molecular Biotechnology. Jena, Germany. "Molecules of Life." Available online. URL: http://www.imb-jena.de/IMAGE.html. Accessed on February 20, 2004.

Karolinska Institutet University Library. Stockholm, Sweden. "Bacterial Infections and Mycoses." Available online. URL: http://www.mic.ki.se/Diseases/C01.html. Accessed on February 20, 2004.

Krstic, R. V. *Illustrated Encyclopedia of Human History.* New York: Springer-Verlag, 1984.

Lentz, Thomas L. *Cell Fine Structure: An Atlas of Drawings of Whole-Cell Structure.* Philadelphia: Saunders, 1971.

Mader, Sylvia S. *Inquiry into Life.* Boston: McGraw-Hill, 2003.

Margulis, L., and K. V. Schwartz. *Five Kingdoms: An illustrated Guide to Phyla of Life on Earth.* New York: Freeman, 1998.

Museum of Paleontology. University of California, Berkeley. "Bacteria: Life History and Ecology." Available online. URL: http://www.ucmp.berkeley.edu/bacteria/bacterialh.html. Accessed on February 20, 2004.

Royal British Columbia Museum. Victoria, British Columbia. "Taxing Problems." An article about the natural history of sea cucumbers. Available online. URL: http://rbcm1.rbcm.gov.bc.ca/nh_papers/taxing.html. Accessed on February 20, 2004.

WEB SITES

The Department of Energy Human Genome Project (United States). Covers every aspect of the human genome project with extensive color illustrations. http://www.ornl.gov/TechResources/Human_ Genome. Accessed on October 9, 2003.

The United States Food and Drug Administration. Provides extensive coverage of general health issues and regulations. http://www.fda. gov. Accessed on October 9, 2003.

Genetic Science Learning Center at the Eccles Institute of Human Genetics, University of Utah. An excellent resource for beginning students. This site contains information and illustrations covering basic cell biology, animal cloning, gene therapy, and stem cells. http://gslc.genetics.utah.edu. Accessed on October 9, 2003.

Institute of Molecular Biotechnology, Jena/Germany. Image library of biological macromolecules. http://www.imb-jena.de/IMAGE. html. Accessed on October 9, 2003.

National Center for Biotechnology Information (NCBI). This site, established by the National Institutes of Health, is an excellent resource for anyone interested in biology. The NCBI provides access to GenBank (DNA sequences), literature databases (Medline and others), molecular databases, and topics dealing with genomic biology. With the literature database, for example, anyone can access Medline's 11 million biomedical journal citations to research biomedical questions. Many of these links provide free access to full-length research papers. http://www.ncbi.nlm.nih.gov. Accessed on October 9, 2003.

The National Human Genome Research Institute (United States). The institute supports genetic and genomic research, including the ethical, legal, and social implications of genetics research. http:// www.genome.gov. Accessed on October 9, 2003.

National Institutes of Health (NIH, United States). The NIH posts information on their Web site that covers a broad range of topics, including general health information, cell biology, aging, cancer research, and much more. http://www.nih.gov. Accessed on October 9, 2003.

Nature. The journal *Nature* provides a comprehensive guide to the human genome. This site presents links to the definitive historical record for the sequences and analyses of human chromosomes. All papers, free for downloading, are based on the final draft produced by the Human Genome Project. http://www.nature.com/nature/focus/humangenome/. Accessed on October 9, 2003.

The Sanger Institute (United Kingdom). DNA sequencing center, named after Fred Sanger, inventor of the most commonly used method for sequencing DNA. The institute is also involved in projects that apply human DNA sequence data to find cures for cancer and other medical disorders. http:/www.sanger.ac.uk. Accessed on October 9, 2003.

INDEX